THE
MUSLIM
WORLD

To Ali, Hossein and Sara, with love

SUTTON POCKET HISTORIES

THE MUSLIM WORLD

COLIN TURNER

SUTTON PUBLISHING

First published in the United Kingdom in 2000 by
Sutton Publishing Limited · Phoenix Mill
Thrupp · Stroud · Gloucestershire · GL5 2BU

British Library Cataloguing in Publication Data
A catalogue record for this book is available from the British
Library.

ISBN 0-7509-2247-8

*Cover illustration: A court scene (reproduced courtesy of the British
Library, London)*

Typeset in 10/13 pt Baskerville.
Typesetting and origination by
Sutton Publishing Limited.
Printed in Great Britain by
The Guernsey Press Company Limited,
Guernsey, Channel Islands.

Contents

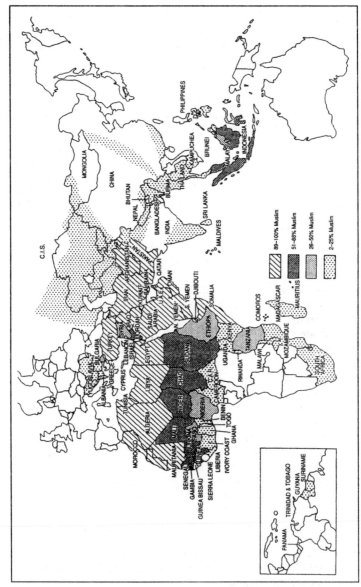

The Peoples of Islam. (From John L. Esposito, *Islam the Straight Path*, OUP, 1988. Reproduced by kind permission)

List of Dates

680	Martyrdom of Husayn at Karbala.
684	Marwanid branch of the Ummayad clan assume control of the caliphate.
692	Defeat of Ibn Zubayr in Mecca; completion of Dome of the Rock in Jerusalem, first great monument of Islamic architecture.
705	Second wave of Arab expansion begins under the caliph Walid.
711	Arabs cross from Maghrib to Gibraltar.
718	Arab siege of Constantinople repulsed.
732	Muslims advance through Europe as far as Tours in north-west France.
732	Muslims defeated by Charles Martel at the Battle of Poitiers.
750	The Abbasid revolt against Ummayad rule takes place; Abbasid dynasty established.
756	The Ummayad 'Abd al-Rahman established himself as sole ruler of Andalusia.
760	Arabs adopt Indian numerals and develop algebra and trigonometry.
762	Baghdad built by the caliph Mansur.
786	Harun al-Rashid becomes caliph; Abbasid dynasty at its zenith.
800	Aghlabids establish themselves as independent rulers of Tunisia (to 909).
809	Death of Harun al-Rashid.
819	Samanids take control of eastern Iran (819–1005).
864	Zaydis take control as independent rulers of the Caspian littoral (to 928).
868	Tulunids establish independent rule in Cairo (to 906).
909	Fatimids establish independent caliphate in north Africa (to 972).
921	'Abd al-Rahman III declares himself caliph in Andalusia, thus breaking away from central caliphate in Baghdad.
945	Shi'ite Buyid family take control of Baghdad; Abbasid caliphs lose effectual power.
969	Fatimids conquer Egypt and found Cairo.
1020	Death of Ferdowsi, writer of the Persian national epic, *Shahnameh*.

1037 Death of Avicenna, Persian philosopher.
1055 Baghdad captured by Seljuks.
1056 Almoravids conquer North Africa and southern Spain.
1066 First Islamic university or nizamiyyeh established.
1071 Battle of Manzikert: defeat of Byzantium by Seljuk Turks.
1091 Imam Ghazali, classical Islam's most illustrious thinker, becomes head of Baghdad nizamiyyeh.
1095 First Crusade begins: Franks invade Anatolia and Syria, and found Crusader states.
1099 Crusaders recapture Jerusalem.
1100 Omar Khayyam composes the Rubaiyyat.
1111 Death of Imam Ghazali.
1135 Almohads dominant in north-western Africa and Muslim Spain.
1144 Second Crusade.
1171 Saladin defeats Fatimids and conquers Egypt.
1188 Saladin destroys Frankish Crusader kingdoms.
1189 Third Crusade.
1202 Fourth Crusade.
1220 Mongol forces capture Samarkand and Bukhara.
1258 Baghdad sacked by the Mongols; the Abbasid dynasty comes to an end.
1299 Ottoman Turks begin expansion in Anatolia.
1326 Ottoman forces capture Bursa in Anatolia.
1366 Edirne established by Ottomans as their European capital.
1392 Taymur-I Lang begins his conquest of Persia; death of Hafiz, Persian lyric poet.
1453 Ottomans capture Constantinople, henceforth known as Istanbul.
1501 Ismail I proclaims himself shah of Iran at Tabriz; Shi'ism becomes the state religion.
1520 Sulayman the Magnificent becomes ruler of the Ottoman empire.
1530 Establishment of Moghul rule in India.
1533 Ottomans capture Baghdad.

1555	Treaty of Amasya marks the end of Perso-Ottoman hostilities.
1556	Akbar the Great comes to power in Moghul India.
1566	Death of Sulayman the Magnficient.
1587	'Abbas I ascends the Safavid throne.
1598	Isfahan becomes the Safavid capital.
1600	British East India Company established.
1605	Death of Moghul ruler, Akbar the Great.
1629	Death of Shah 'Abbas I of Iran.
1699	Treaty of Karlowitz; Ottomans forced to surrended territory in Balkans.
1718	Treaty of Passarowtiz: Ottomans forced to surrender Serbia.
1722	Isfahan falls to Sunni Afghan forces.
1736	Nadir Shah becomes ruler of Iran.
1739	Nadir Shah captures Delhi.
1744	Revivalist leader 'Abd al-Wahhab joins forces with Muhammad b. Saud.
1764	British become rulers of Bengal; Moghul rule on the decline.
1794	Qajar dynasty established in Iran.
1798	Napoleon occupies Egypt.
1839	Ottomans begin Tanzimat reforms, the first attempts at modernization in the Muslim world.
1884	Britain becomes *de facto* ruler of Egypt.
1905	Constitutional revolution in Iran.
1917	Balfour Declaration promises Jews a national home in Palestine.
1922	Egypt declared independent monarchy under Fuad I.
1922	Palestine comes under British mandate.
1923	Ottoman caliphate comes to an end.
1928	Muslim Brotherhood founded by Hasan al-Banna.
1932	Saudia Arabia comes into existence under Abdul Aziz ibn Saud.
1932	Iraq becomes independent state.
1941	Islamic Society founded in Pakistan by Maududi.
1945	Syria becomes charter member of the UN.
1946	Jordan and Lebanon gain independence.

1947   Partition of India and creation of Pakistan.

1948   The state of Israel created on Palestinian soil; first Arab-Israeli war.

1948   Muslim Brotherhood outlawed in Egypt.

1949   Indonesia gains independence.

1951   Libya becomes independent monarchy.

1952   King Farouk of Egypt overthrown by Gamal Abdul Nasser.

1956   Tunisia, Morocco and Sudan become independent; second Arab-Israeli war.

1956   Suez crisis: Anglo-French invasion of canal zone.

1957   Malaya gains independence.

1960   Mali, Mauritania, Niger, Nigeria, Somalia and Upper Volta gain independence.

1962   Algeria gains independence.

1963   Anti-government unrest in Iran leads to exile of leading cleric, Ayatullah Khumayni.

1967   Third Arab-Israeli war.

1971   Indo-Pakistan war leads to breakaway of East Pakistan (Bangladesh).

1973   Fourth Arab-Israeli war.

1977   Egypt/Israeli peace talks culminating in Camp David Peace Treaty.

1979   Khumayni returns to Iran to lead Islamic revolution; Russia invades Afghanistan.

1981   President Sadat of Egypt assassinated by Muslim 'fundamentalists'.

1982   Israel invades Lebanon.

1989   Ayatullah Khumayni dies.

Introduction

It has often been said that it is only through knowing the past that we can begin to truly understand the present, and the past of the Muslim world is clearly no exception. The world of Islam and the global community of Muslims constitute an increasingly important part of our mental landscape, and to understand something – however general and limited in scope – about the past which has shaped them adds to our comprehension of the Muslim present. It is with this aim in mind that *The Muslim World* has been written.

ONE

The Formative Era

PRE-ISLAMIC ARABIA

'When the legend becomes fact,' someone once said, 'print the legend.' The history of Islam and the Muslim world is no stranger to legends, some more persistent than others. The old idea that Islam is a religion of the desert, designed for a desert mind-set, is one; the notion that it was spread by the sword is another. Almost as deep-rooted is the popular assumption that the appearance of Islam was coterminous with that of the Arabs, and that prior to the advent of Muhammad they had little history to speak of. Yet Islam did not emerge into a vacuum; nor was its founder, and the society of which he was part, without a past. It is to this past – the history of pre-Islamic Arabia – that we must first turn if we are to contextualize the coming of Islam and the genesis of Muslim civilization.

Our story begins in the sixth century in the vast Arabian peninsula, an area of mainly rock and desert some 700 miles wide and over 1,000 long. Those who lived there did so under the harshest of physical conditions, scorched for most of the year by a relentless sun which made survival something of an achievement. Yet on its coasts were dotted numerous small ports, home to Arab seafarers who were known throughout the region as men of enterprise, forming an important part of the trade network which linked India and Mesopotamia to East Africa, Egypt and the Mediterranean. Also, for several hundred years before, and for a century after, the birth of Christ, the southern part of Arabia had been the locus of several prosperous kingdoms, with civil institutions as advanced as any in the world at that time. However, a variety of socioeconomic factors led to gradual changes in the population structure; among them, according to later Muslim historians, the bursting of the great dam of Ma'rib in the Yemen. Consequently, the inhabitants were forced to migrate northwards. There, untouched by the civilizing influence of the two great empires of the region, Byzantium and Persia, the migrants formed a tribal society based on pastoral nomadism, thus creating the Arabia of Muhammad's day.

Some Arabian tribes were involved in trade between the Mediterannean and the southern seas, ferrying goods on that trusty 'ship of the desert', the ubiquitous camel, between the commercial centres of Syria and the southern port of Aden. A large number, however, made a precarious living out of raiding other tribes or plundering trade caravans, or by herding camels, sheep and goats in a life led constantly on the move, as they searched out fresh pastures from oasis to oasis. If such a picture tends to reinforce the old image of the 'uncivilized Bedouin', then it is most misleading, for in fact desert life was lived to the highest of values. Qualities such as manliness, valour, generosity and hospitality were valued highly; even the intertribal raids, and the vendettas which occurred whenever blood was shed, were conducted according to precise, if unwritten, rules. The Arabs were also lovers of poetry, producing a literature that was communicated orally from father to son, and from tribe to tribe. Even those who eventually became settled in the oasis towns took their tribal values with them, fiercely proud of their heritage as free men of the desert.

By the end of the sixth century, certain changes had begun to occur. At some oases the population was growing, and with it the development of sedentary life. The town of Mecca was one such oasis. Situated at the junction of two major trade routes, it had enjoyed a certain amount of prestige since ancient times. More important than its prestige as a commercial centre, however, was its prominence as the sacred city of the desert Arabs – a status it still enjoys, albeit under very different circumstances.

The Arabs were polytheists, believing in nature gods and goddesses, demons and spirits. The focus of their worship was a cubic structure, the *ka'ba*, situated in the middle of Mecca and originally built, so later Muslims claimed, by the prophet Abraham. Around the *ka'ba* stood a whole panoply of effigies – traditionally 360 in number – to which the Arabs would make sacrifices; once a year, this pantheon of gods was witness to a ritual pilgrimage, which would later be Islamicized by Muhammad as the annual *hajj*. Apart from offering the Arabs a focal point for identification with their objects of worship, the pagan pilgrimage was also an important source of income for the Meccans, who saw their city emerge as the most prosperous in the peninsula.

With prosperity, however, there came tension, as the hitherto unquestioned loyalties of tribal structure were called into question by the demands of commerce. As Mecca grew more prosperous, the divide between rich and poor increased. Later Muslim historians tell of a city in which the old tribal values had been abandoned, and in which a dog-eat-dog culture prevailed, fuelled by greed and envy. It was into this milieu that Muhammad, founder of Islam, emerged.

MUHAMMAD AND THE ADVENT OF ISLAM

Born in the year 570, Muhammad belonged to the Banu Hashim, a comparatively poor but well-respected clan of the Quraysh tribe, the most esteemed and influential in Mecca. His father, Abdullah, died before Muhammad was born; his mother, Amina, passed away when the young boy was barely six. From that point onwards, Muhammad was cared for by his grandfather, 'Abd al-Muttalib.

Of Muhammad's formative years, little is known. By his early twenties it seems that he was a seasoned participant in Meccan commercial life, having accompanied his older male relatives on trading missions throughout the peninsula and beyond. His reputation for fairness – his nickname was al-Amin, or 'the trustworthy one' – was well known among his peers, and it was probably this trait above all others that brought him to the attention of a prominent Meccan widow named Khadija. She duly hired him to manage her business affairs and, impressed by his impeccable conduct, later proposed to him. Muhammad's marriage to Khadija, who was his senior by fifteen years, was by his own admission possibly the happiest and most influential of all his unions. At this point in his career there was no outward sign in either his character or his

circumstances to suggest that his life would be anything but
ordinary, at least in the context of seventh-century Mecca. But
all this was to change. And the change, when it came, was to
transform Muhammad – and history – beyond recognition.

According to the Islamic *hadith*[1] literature, Muhammad had
always been a serious, introspective youth who was never at
ease with the pagan values of Meccan society. Muslim
hagiographers claim that he had denounced polytheism at an
early age, adopting the outlook of the fabled monotheistic
recluses, the *hanifs*, who believed in one God yet adhered
neither to Christianity nor Judaism. Other stories describe
how, during a trading mission to Syria, the young Muhammad
had been singled out by a Christian monk as one destined for
prophethood. What is more or less certain, however, is that, in
keeping with pagan tradition, he was given to long bouts of
isolated meditation, during which he would ponder the
mysteries of human existence and pray for guidance. It was
during one of these retreats, in a cave on nearby Mount Hira,
that Muhammad, then in his fortieth year, received his first
calling. A vision – later identified by Muhammad as the
archangel Gabriel – appeared, saying: 'Recite! In the name of
thy Lord and Cherisher, who created – created man, out of a
(mere) clot of congealed blood; Recite! And thy Lord is Most
Bountiful – He Who taught (the use of) the Pen – taught man
that which he knew not.'[2]

Initially Muhammad was terrified by the experience,
convinced that he had been visited by demons. However,
Khadija reassured him that this was not the case, and as the
visions continued, Muhammad's faith in his new prophetic
mission increased. The source of the messages, he concluded,

was not the devil but God Himself – the same God who had revealed himself to Abraham, to Moses and to Jesus before him.

As the revelations continued, Muhammad began to preach them to his closest relatives. Khadija, his beloved wife, became his first follower; Ali, his young cousin, his second.

The message vouchsafed in the revelations, which later came to be known as the Koran (Arabic *qur'an*, or 'recitation'), was clear: there is only one God, and Muhammad is His messenger. The whole of the created realm – the cosmos – belongs to Him and Him alone, and man, as the pinnacle of God's creation, has been put on earth to realize this. Man's earthly life is thus but a test, in which he must strive to know, love and worship God as He has intended. And at the end of his earthly life, man will stand before the divine tribunal on the Day of Judgement. For those who come to believe in God, submit their wills to His and perform good works, heaven awaits; for those who ignore God's message and submit to no will but their own, the flames of hellfire lie in ambush.

As Muhammad himself asserted, the new religion, Islam, was nothing novel. Indeed, he declared, God had sent countless prophets to other communities in the past with the same message: believe in one God, the judgement of the Last Day, and reform yourselves and your society before it is too late. Having failed to heed the words of their prophets, however, their communities had been destroyed. And so now Muhammad had been commanded to rise up with his own message, the Koran, which he claimed would be the last scripture revealed by God before the end of time, while Muhammad himself would be the final prophet.[3]

6

At first, Muhammad confined his mission to his closest relatives, but after a year or two he was instructed by God to declare his prophethood openly. Initially his claims were met with derision: either he had gone mad, his fellow Meccans concluded, or he was merely repeating what he had heard from the Jews and Christians he had met on his travels. Their beliefs were, after all, not unheard of in the peninsula. Clearly he was making it all up. Soon, however, derision turned to anger as Muhammad began to inveigh in earnest against the polytheism of his fellow tribesmen and blame their greed, envy and licentiousness for all of society's ills.

In attacking the gods of the *ka'ba*, Muhammad was threatening not only the belief system of his peers but also the economic heart of Meccan society. Furthermore, he advocated social reform on a vast scale, with measures sanctioned by the Koran to improve the position of slaves, orphans, women and the poor. It was clear, therefore, that the pagans of Mecca had to act. Muhammad himself was out of their reach; when his grandfather died, he had been taken under the wing of his uncle, Abu Talib, a respected member of the community who afforded him protection. The pagans – mostly the rich merchants who ruled the town – began therefore to persecute Muhammad's growing band of followers. The oppression became so great that in 615, Muhammad was forced to send some eighty families of converts to a safe haven in Ethiopia. Then, when both Khadija and Abu Talib died in the same year, Muhammad himself came under attack. In despair Muhammad fled to the coastal town of Taif for help, but to no avail. Shortly afterwards, however, a delegation of men arrived in Mecca from Yathrib, an oasis town 200 miles to the north that was riven by intertribal feuding. Having learned of Muhammad's reputation for fairness, they asked him to arbitrate between the feuding parties. In return, they vowed to pledge allegiance to him as prophet. Muhammad accepted, and began almost immediately to send his followers on to safety in Yathrib.

Muhammad was the last to escape Mecca and certain death, arriving in Yathrib a week later. The exodus of Muslim believers was known as the *hijra* (lit. 'migration'), and was later used to mark the beginning of the Islamic calendar. Those followers who emigrated with him became known as the *muhajirun* (lit. 'migrants'), while the people of Yathrib who promised him shelter and support came to be known as the *ansar*, or 'helpers'.

In Yathrib, which was later renamed Medina (from the Arabic *madinat al-rasool*, or 'city of the Prophet'), Muhammad turned his attention to the formation of a community, or *umma*, which was to based on the social regulations revealed in the Koran and which would have at its heart not loyalty to the tribe, as had been the case in pre-Islamic Mecca, but a common belief in one God. In this community of believers, everyone was equal in the sight of God. Even those who believed not in the Koran but in the Torah and Gospel which preceded it had a place in the new scheme of things, as laid down in one of the world's oldest political documents, the famous 'Constitution of Medina'. In this, Muhammed outlined the rights and duties of all citizens, with the Jews of Medina recognized as a separate but equal community, with complete freedom to practise their own religion. As Muhammad gave shape to the new community, fresh revelations appeared from

God to aid him in his task. It is not surprising, therefore, that many of the verses revealed in the Medinan stage of the Prophet's career are legislative in nature, containing guidance on practical matters such as prayer and fasting, marriage and divorce, buying and selling, taxation and inheritance. Islam the religion of personal submission to the will of God was now externalized as Islam the collective submission of the community.

Yet while Muhammad was busy building his community state, Meccan hostility to the new movement in Medina was increasing, with the Meccans calling for the extradition of Muhammad and those who had emigrated along with him, the *muhajirun*. Muhammad's cause was not helped by the presence in Medina of a group of individuals who, while nominally embracing Islam, secretly opposed it and worked actively for its downfall. Known as the *munafiqun*, or 'hypocrites', this group was to remain a thorn in Muhammad's side for the rest of his career. The *munafiqun* in turn were aided by three of the Jewish tribes, whom eventually Muhammad was forced to punish with exile and, in one case, mass execution.

As the threat from Mecca worsened, Muhammad embarked on a strategy of 'defence through attack', and began to raid the Meccan trade caravans as they returned from Syria. This led to the first major encounter at Badr, just outside Medina, in 624. The battle of Badr was a psychological turning point for the Muslims. Outnumbered three to one, they saw their decisive victory over the Meccans as ample proof that God was on their side; opportunely, Muhammad received a fresh revelation from God to confirm their victory, which he attributed to God's succour rather than their own exertions.

The Muslims' elation after Badr was quickly dispelled, however, when they were defeated by the Meccans a year later at the battle of Uhud. Apparently, the zeal of some Muslims had been such that they had ignored the Prophet's advice on battle strategy and rushed recklessly into the fray, eager for victory and the spoils which went with it; the Prophet himself was wounded and God, in yet another timely revelation, rebuked the Muslims for their rashness. Meccan leadership, though, was hopelessly disunited, and thus the pagans were unable to make their victory a decisive one by capturing Medina and overthrowing the nascent Islamic regime.

Finally, in 627, the Meccans tried again. With an army of some ten thousand men, they subjected Medina to a siege, but were unable to take the city. The Battle of the Ditch – so called because one of Muhammad's Persian followers had dug a trench around the city to foil the Meccan cavalry – culminated in a resounding victory for the Muslims, and the Meccans, who soon ran out of food and water, were forced to return to Mecca. Meanwhile, Muhammad eliminated those groups in Medina which had either sympathized with, or actively supported, the Meccan invaders. Following each of the battles of Badr and Uhud he had banished a Jewish tribe and confiscated its property; after the Battle of the Ditch he had all of the women and children of the third Jewish tribe taken into slavery, and the males of the tribe massacred.

Fully aware that they were no match for Medina, the Meccans had no choice but to accept Muhammad's offer of a truce. The Treaty of Hudaybah, concluded in 628, marked a cessation of hostilities, and stipulated that the Muslims be allowed to make their pilgrimage to Mecca the following year.

In 630, after some of the Meccans had been accused of breaking the treaty, Muhammad marched on his birthplace with an army of ten thousand Muslims. The Meccans surrendered, accepting Muhammad's leadership and submitting en masse to the new religion. Muhammad had come home, and Islam had come home with him.

As news of the conquest of Mecca spread, delegations poured in from all over the peninsula, with tribe after tribe converting to Islam and declaring their allegiance to the Prophet. By the time of his death in June 632, virtually the entire population of Arabia had become Muslim.

THE 'RIGHTLY GUIDED' CALIPHS

With the death of the founder of Islam, the nascent Muslim community was plunged into crisis. Muhammad the Prophet was gone, and the Koran made it quite clear that no other messenger would rise after him: as God's final revelation, the Koran would suffice mankind until the end of time. What the Koran did not elucidate was the issue of temporal authority. Who was to succeed Muhammad as political leader of the *umma*, and how was he to be chosen?

Most of his followers believed that Muhammad, like the Koran, had remained silent on the subject, neither appointing a successor nor proposing any particular form of election process for the future. However, some claimed that the Prophet had chosen Ali to succeed him; the latter's supporters were known as the *shi'at*, or 'party', of Ali, later evolving into the Shi'ites. The schism which emerged between this group and the majority of Muslims, known as the Sunnites

11

(those who adhere to the Prophet's path or *sunna*), continues to this day.

Regardless of whether or not Muhammad did appoint a successor, Ali did not become the first leader of the Muslim community after the death of the Prophet. The title of caliph (from the Arabic *khalifa*, meaning 'deputy of God') went instead to Muhammad's father-in-law and close companion, Abu Bakr, who was elected in Ali's absence by a small committee of elders. Abu Bakr was to be the first of four successors to Muhammad later known as the *rashidun*, or 'rightly guided' caliphs, largely on account of their status as close companions of the Prophet and their reputation as men of piety and justice.

On becoming caliph, Abu Bakr's first challenge was to put down the tribal insurrections which had begun to spring up throughout the peninsula after the Prophet's death. It appeared that many of the Bedouin tribes who had converted to Islam during Muhammad's lifetime had done so for political reasons only; now that he was dead, they deemed what they considered to be their part of the 'pact' null and void, and so began to abandon Islam in droves. Aware that such a revolt threatened the future of the community-state, Abu Bakr moved against the tribes and, in a series of encounters which came to be known as the 'wars of apostasy', crushed the insurrectionists in 633. By the time of his death a year later, peace and stability had been restored to the peninsula.

Shortly before he died in 634, Abu Bakr designated another of the Prophet's close companions, Umar, to succeed him. Although the appointment was opposed by the supporters of Ali, who were outraged that their candidate had been passed over for a second time, Umar met with little internal resistance during his ten years in office. Shortly after succeeding to the post, Umar added the honorific *amir al-mu'minin* ('commander of the faithful') to that of caliph, denoting the fact that leadership of the community was spiritual as well as political; from then on, all caliphs used the same title.

Yet it is for his military leadership rather than his role as spiritual guide that Umar is remembered, and not without justification. For it was Umar who presided over one of the most amazing feats of territorial expansion and empire building that history has ever witnessed: a wave of conquests that, within twelve years of the Prophet's death, would enable the Muslim community-state of Medina to overthrow the Persian empire and conquer all of the eastern Mediterranean territories of the Roman empire apart from Anatolia. The rapidity and comparative ease with which this first wave of conquests was carried out perplexes historians to this day.

Umar's first conquests were in Syria, with Byzantium losing Damascus to the Muslim forces in 635; Jerusalem, a city sacred to Jews, Christians and Muslims alike, was captured two years later. Meanwhile, as Syria was being invaded to the west, Muslim forces were also busy in the east, marching through Iraq in an attempt to bring down the Sassanid empire of Persia. The Sassanids, already weakened following a recent defeat to the Byzantines, were no match for the invaders, and in 637 the Muslim forces scored a famous victory at Qadisiyya, near the Euphrates. From there the Muslims moved eastwards and occupied Ctesiphon, the Sassanid capital. By 641 the Sassanids had relinquished all of their lands to the west of the Zagros mountains.

With Ctesiphon secured, the Muslims turned west once more, this time into Egypt. In 641 the ancient fortress of Babylon, south of present-day Cairo, was captured; the following year Alexandria fell. Three years later the Byzantines recaptured the city, but their stay was brief: it was reclaimed by the Muslims the following year, and the Christians never ruled in Egypt again. With the fall of Alexandria to the Muslims in 645, the first wave of Muslim conquests came to an end. During his ten-year rule Umar had succeeded in conquering a vast swathe of territories surrounding the Arabian peninsula: Syria, Egypt, Iraq and much of Persia, thus creating what was at that time the second largest empire in the world, only slightly smaller than that of China. From its humble beginnings in a cave outside Mecca, Islam, the galvanizing force behind the conquests, had now become a major player on the world stage.

Realizing that their loyalty was crucial to the success of the new Islamic empire, Umar made sure that his new subjects were not oppressed by the invading forces, and that their lives were not disrupted unduly by the change of regime. This involved leaving things, where possible, very much as they had been under previous administrations. In Syria, for example, the old civil service of the Byzantines was retained until Umar was able to establish his own system, and thus Greek remained the language of administration for another half-century; a similar situation obtained in Muslim Persia. The caliph also tried not to burden the conquered peoples with excess taxation; to this end, he introduced the *kharaj*, or 'land tax', levied on farmers in accordance with the productivity of their fields. The conquered peoples were also allowed to carry on practising their own religion, albeit upon payment of a kind of poll tax known as the *jizya*. Thus the old legend that Islam was spread by the sword is not borne out by history; if anything, the Muslims avoided proselytizing, aware that attempts at conversion would rob the caliphal coffers of an important source of revenue. Moreover, in the first few decades after the conquests, the invading Arab soldiers were separated from the local populace in specially built garrison towns – such as Basra in Iraq, and Fustat in Egypt – where they were encouraged to keep to themselves. Later on, of course, assimilation did occur, and with it, conversion. However, those who became Muslim did so of their own accord, sometimes sincerely, sometimes for financial gain, but never under duress.

After Umar's death in 644 the caliphate fell to Uthman, a scion of the Umayyad family, who was elected by a council of Muhammad's companions. Although he later proved to be a man of considerable piety and good character, he was not considered the strongest candidate for the job and hence lacked unanimous support: the supporters of Ali, who had been campaigning for his right to succeed Muhammad ever since the latter's death, were particularly resentful that he had been overlooked for a third time.

Under Uthman (644–56) the empire continued to grow, although not at the breakneck pace it had enjoyed under his immediate predecessor. Nevertheless, his military exploits were not without import. In 645 his forces stymied the Byzantine attempt to recapture Alexandria, after which Uthman was able to advance further into North Africa. The creation of the first Muslim fleet, designed to guard the Mediterranean against Byzantine naval attacks, was another achievement; it also helped him to conquer the island of Cyprus in 649. And to the east, Uthman completed Umar's conquest of Persia by occupying the strategically important province of Khorasan, the 'grain basket' of the old Sassanian empire, in 653.

At home, Uthman's most important undertaking was his attempt to establish the definitive version of the Koran. Up until then, several variant readings had been in circulation, with learned Muslims unable to agree on the correct manner of Koranic recitation. The disputes which ensued were deemed serious enough to damage the integrity of the holy book, and so Uthman decided to act. Summoning three of Muhammad's most trustworthy companions, he ordered them to make perfect copies of the first complete written manuscript of the Koran, which had been handed down from Abu Bakr to Umar and from Umar to his daughter, Hafsa. Their task completed, the companions were then instructed to send identical copies to all four corners of the nascent Muslim empire to replace the contentious material. The text which emerged as a result is the one which exists today.

Sadly for Uthman, however, it is for his political ineptitude that he is most remembered. His reign saw a decrease in the treasury – a result, it was claimed, of the kind of lavish spending that was highly inappropriate for a caliph and exemplar. More damaging, though, were the accusations of nepotism levelled against him. Uthman's promotion of his Umayyad kin to positions of power and influence in the caliphal administration engendered much controversy, helping to create a climate of general discontent that led ultimately to his downfall. As Medina became the scene of popular unrest, supported by disaffected Egyptian soldiers, Uthman was murdered in June 656.

After Uthman's death Ali finally succeeded to the caliphate, establishing himself in the Iraqi city of Kufa where he enjoyed most support. Almost immediately, however, he found himself embroiled in the first civil war in the community's history. The main struggle was between the new caliph's supporters, the *shi'at Ali* (lit. 'party of Ali') or Shi'ites, and those who refused to recognize his new status. Foremost among the latter was Mu'awiya, Uthman's Umayyad cousin and governor of Syria. Incensed that Ali seemed unwilling to punish Uthman's assassins, Mu'awiya and his family challenged the new caliph's leadership, declaring it unlawful. Ali's election was also disputed by two of the Prophet's companions, Talha and Zubayr, and one of the Prophet's widows, the redoubtable 'Aisha, whose coolness towards Ali had a long history. The first physical confrontation between Ali and his detractors came in December 656 at the so-called 'Battle of the Camel' near the garrison town of Basra; Talha and Zubayr were killed, while 'Aisha was returned to Medina.

Ali then turned his attention to the Syrian problem, at the heart of which lay Mu'awiya himself. Mu'awiya had by this time been governor in Damascus for almost twenty years. As the son of the infamous Abu Sufyan, he had inherited the leadership of the Umayyads and was thus in command of possibly the largest and most efficient personal army in the Muslim world at that time. He also enjoyed the unquestioning support of the Syrian Arabs, who recognized him as the only legitimate successor to the murdered Uthman. Ali's task would, by his own admission, not be an easy one. In 657 the two forces met at Siffin on the upper Euphrates. The outcome was more disastrous than Ali could ever have imagined. As the battle drew near to its inconclusive end, Mu'awiya's troops hit upon a strategy that was as brilliant as it was perfidious: tearing leaves from the Koran, they thrust them aloft on their spears, called a halt to the fighting, and entreated Ali and his forces to 'let God decide between us'. Disoriented by this spectacle, Ali agreed to arbitration. His supporters, however, did not lend him unanimous backing. A large group of them broke away from him, outraged that Ali should put the fate of the community in the hands of a human tribunal rather than vanquish the dissident Umayyads in battle as God had surely intended. They later became known as the Kharijites (lit. 'those who secede'), with their own movement, theology and distinct political ethos. Ali later dealt a severe blow to the Kharijites at the battle of Nahrawan in 658, but was unable to break their spirit, as later events were to prove.

Meanwhile, the arbitration having proved inconclusive, Mu'awiya proclaimed himself caliph in July 660, thus further undermining Ali's leadership. With the support of the governor of Egypt, as well as his loyal Syrian forces, he was even able to order raids on Ali's base in Iraq. More important, however, was the unexpected assistance he received from the Kharijites, whose defeat at Nahrawan had transformed them into a militant organization. For it was one of their number who, early in 661, stole into Ali's apartments as the latter sat in prayer. With one stroke of the sword it was all over: Ali fell, and with him the era of the 'rightly guided' caliphs came to an ignominious end.

Despite the troubles which beset the caliphates of Uthman and Ali, Muslims still look back to the period of the 'rightly-guided' caliphs as the golden age of Islam and Islamic rule. It was, after all, the era for them in which God's final message to mankind found expression in the creation of an Islamic community-state, held together by ties of religious commitment and solidarity. It was the era in which the definitive reading of the Koran had emerged, ensuring that God's revelation would be preserved for all men at all times and forming the basis for the later development of the Islamic sciences of jurisprudence and theology. And above all it was the era of the Arab conquests, which took Islam halfway round the known world, thus validating its message in the eyes of the believers.

TWO

The Classical Era

THE UMAYYADS

After Ali's death, Mu'awiya took over the caliphate, thus founding the Umayyad dynasty, and moved the capital to Damascus. This change of capital signified more than simply a change of ruler: it was emblematic of a profound change in the social philosophy, religious outlook and cultural orientation of the Islamic community-state. Under the 'rightly guided' caliphs, religious faith had a determining role in the unification of society, and was the chief motivation of the individual in his social life. Under the Umayyads, religious faith counted for little. Blood and tribal relations once again resurfaced to become the chief motivating principle between the social groups.

The Umayyad state had two related branches: the Sufyanids (661–84) and the Marwanids (684–750). Of the three Sufyanids, only Mu'awiya achieved anything of note. Under his leadership, the army was modernized and the empire continued to expand; to govern the conquered lands more efficiently, Mu'awiya introduced divans, or registries, and an effective postal system. In an overt move back to a more tribal style of leadership, he revived the old practices of *shura*

20

(a council of tribal elders) and *wufud* (a delegation sent by tribes to keep the caliph informed of their interests). It is the adoption of such institutions that leads many of his critics to describe Mu'awiya not as caliph but as *malik*, or tribal king in the style of the pre-Islamic rulers of southern Arabia.

Proof that Mu'awiya saw himself as king rather than caliph finally came when he named his inept and licentious son, Yazid, as his successor. Outraged at the thought of the leadership of the Muslim community falling into the hands of one so morally bankrupt, many refused to pay allegiance. In Medina the old Muslim families rallied around Abdullah ibn Zubayr, son of one of Muhammad's closest companions, as he rose up in revolt. At the same time the people of Kufa, Ali's former capital, sent a delegation to Ali's son, Husayn, inviting him to spearhead their revolt against Yazid. Husayn, who had never acknowledged the new caliph, accepted. He duly set out for Kufa with a small band of relatives and companions, whereupon the governor of Iraq, on behalf of Yazid, sent an army of four thousand men to intercept them. The commander of the army demanded their surrender, but Husayn refused, adamant that he would never give in to a caliph whose authority he did not recognize. And so, in October 680, on the plain of Karbala near the banks of the Euphrates, Husayn and most of those with him were brutally massacred. Husayn's head was severed from his body and despatched to Yazid in Damascus. Muslim historians describe how even the tyrannical Yazid blanched when he saw how Husayn, the grandson of the Prophet, had been treated. The massacre of Husayn was a turning point in Islamic history, with revenge for Husayn's death becoming a clarion call which helped to weaken the Umayyad government and strengthen the Shi'ite cause. In the process, Husayn was hailed as the symbol of supreme resistance, and the annual remembrance of his martyrdom incorporated into Shi'ite cultic practice.

After the death of the last Sufyanid ruler, Mu'awiya II (d. 684), the caliphate fell to the Marwanid clan, led by Marwan ibn al-Hakam, a cousin of Mu'awiya I and one of the most influential figures of Uthman's caliphate. The transfer of power from one branch to the other occurred not through election, however, but through a bloody encounter at Marj Rahit, to the north of Damascus, between the Qays tribe, which preferred Ibn Zubayr, and the Kalb tribe, which supported Marwan. To eradicate their opponents, the Marwani forces wasted no time in attacking Medina, leaving much destruction in their wake before moving on to besiege Mecca itself.

Under the Marwanids, eleven caliphs ruled the Umayyad state for some seventy years. Among them only four stand out as having achieved anything of lasting significance. Under 'Abd al-Malik, Arabic was introduced for the first time as the language of government administration. New coins were struck and Byzantine and Persian currency replaced by a single system across the empire: the gold *dinar* and the silver *dirham*. Elaborate mosques sprang up and lavish palaces were constructed for the wealthy and influential. But it was for his military zeal that 'Abd al-Malik has found a place in the history books. When he became caliph, Damascus was threatened from Byzantium on one side and from Ibn Zubayr in Mecca on the other. To tackle the problem, he adopted a policy of 'sword and negotiation'. Negotiation was used to resolve his difficulties with Byzantium; consequently, he made several slight territorial concessions to the Bzyantine emperor, to whom he agreed to pay tribute. The sword was used to deal with the internal opposition. With the aid of his lieutenant, the vicious Hajjaj b. Yusuf, he brought Mecca to its knees and finally defeated Ibn Zubayr in 692. In Iraq he subdued the Muslims with what can only be described as a reign of terror. The executions, it is said, proceeded day and night – so many, in fact, that there were not enough executioners to behead the condemned.

'Abd al-Malik was succeeded in 705 by his son, Walid (705–15), under whom the second wave of Arab conquests took place. In north Africa, the Berber tribes were converted en masse to Islam; having accepted the leadership of the Arabs, they then joined forces with them to make the first inroads into the Iberian peninsula. On the eastern front, Muslim forces occupied Sind, where they were welcomed by a Buddhist people discontented with Hindu rule. For many, Walid's reign marked the zenith of Umayyad power. The expansion effected during his reign increased gradually after his death, so that by 732 the Muslim conquerors had advanced as far as the city of Tours in north-west France. Exactly one hundred years after the death of the Prophet, the word of his successors was law from south-western Europe, through north Africa into western and central Asia – an extent unmatched by even the Roman empire at its zenith.

Internally, the strength of the Marwani Umayyads lay chiefly in their ability to manipulate the tribal networks and connections which had resurfaced as a major force in Arab society after the demise of the 'rightly-guided' caliphs. Under the Umayyads, many of the old tribal attitudes and traditions had been revived as Arab clans and tribes established themselves as landowners throughout the growing empire. Faction fighting was one such tradition, and throughout most of the Umayyad period, succession to the caliphate depended on the outcome of the feuds and infighting among rival tribes. The rivalry between the Qays and the Kalb, which persisted throughout the Umayyad era, has already been mentioned.

Another tribal attitude dominant during the Umayyad period was Arabism; for many of the Arab invaders, being an Arab was considered more important than being a Muslim. To an extent this was reflected in the social hierarchy which existed in the conquered territories. At the apex of the pyramid stood the conquerors, the Arab Muslims. Below them came the Muslim converts of the tributary peoples, the 'neo-Muslims', for whom participation in the sociopolitical arena depended on their ability to affiliate themselves as *mawali*, or 'clients', of Arab clans. Then came the 'people of the Book' – the Jews and Christians – who were known to the Arabs as *dhimmis*, or 'protected people'. At the bottom of the pile came the slaves – converted or unconverted – and those who adhered to no revealed religion in particular. Arabism was both a cause and consequence of this divisive social structure, and indeed in many parts of the empire was accepted as a norm sanctioned by Islam itself; and all of this despite the Koranic verses which teach the equality of all men before God.

Walid I was succeeded in 715 by Sulayman, whose two-year reign was frittered away in pursuit of wine, women and song. Succeeding Sulayman, however, was the one exception to the tribally oriented Arab style of government: Umar b. 'Abd al-Aziz, better known as Umar II. Like the 'rightly guided' caliph of the same name, Umar II was a man of great personal piety and humility, whose woefully short reign did much to restore people's faith in the caliphate. He was able to reconcile the warring factions of the time, including the Shi'ites and the Kharijites, and thus right much of the wrong done by his predecessors. Unfortunately, he was succeeded by Sulayman's brother, Yazid III (720–4), who proceeded, with his debauchery and cruelty, to undo much of what Umar had accomplished.

The last Umayyad caliph of note was Hisham (724–43), during whose twenty-year reign the bureaucratic structure of the caliphate was improved and a greater degree of centralization achieved. One of Hisham's more enlightened measures was the use of skilled non-Muslims in the administration. Such was the efficiency of the caliphal machine that Hisham's style of government later became the ideal to which other absolute rulers would aspire. Yet efficiency was to be had at a price, and for many it was a heavy one: Hisham ruled with an iron fist, using arbitrary arrest and torture against anyone who disagreed with him.

The last four Umayyad caliphs were fashioned in the same mould as most of their tyrannical forebears, and accomplished nothing of import during their reigns. Yet even if they had been able to redeem themselves with a series of administrative reforms, or even a spate of monument building, the feeling across the empire was that enough was enough. Disaffection was spreading rapidly throughout the conquered territories, with resentment highest among the new converts to Islam, especially those of non-Arab origin such as the Persians. Other discontented groups included the Shi'ites, for whom the memory of Karbala was an open wound, and the Kharijites, for whom the Umayyads had always been beyond the pale. Khorasan, in eastern Persia, was the main hotbed of unrest, and it was from there, in 750, that the Abbasid revolt against the Umayyad regime began.

THE ABBASIDS

The name Abbasid signifies the descendants of 'Abbas (d. 653), the uncle of the Prophet. The Abbasid family had opposed the Umayyads from the outset, and from the time of the caliph Sulayman (d. 717) had been instrumental in spreading propaganda and fomenting unrest against them. Gradually they won the support of the disaffected Shi'ites and *mawali*, especially those in Khurasan. In 747 a member of the *mawali*, Abu Muslim, rose up in the name of the Abbasids. This led to the defeat of the last Umayyad caliph, Marwan II, and the accession of the first Abbasid caliph, Abu al-'Abbas al-Saffah (749–54).

However, al-Saffah turned out to be no better than his Umayyad predecessors: for five years he ruled as a bloodthirsty tyrant, eradicating many of the leaders who had helped him attain the caliphate, including Abu Muslim. That al-Saffah should have been murdered by his own brother, the equally ruthless al-Mansur (754–75) smacks of poetic justice.

Al-Mansur's crowning accomplishment was the construction of a new capital for the dynasty. Built in 762 on the banks of the Tigris and close to the Euphrates on the main route to Persia, the 'round city' of Baghdad was created by, and for, a ruler who combined the pomp and circumstance of the

Byzantine emperors with the opulence and grandeur of the Sassanian shahs. The position of leader in Islamic society was no longer that of *primus inter pares* – first among equal believers – as it had been during the era of the Prophet and his immediate successors; under the Abbasids, the caliphate acquired a majesty and mystique that owed more to the semi-divine aura attending Persian kingship than it did to the simple ethos of leadership espoused by Muhammad and the 'rightly guided' caliphs, and the new city was designed precisely to accentuate the remoteness of the ruler from his people. Consisting of a series of concentric rings, Baghdad had as its nucleus the palace and private mosques of the caliph and his household; court offices and military barracks formed the outer, protective ring, while the markets and residential quarters constituted the periphery. Whereas the early caliphs had prided themselves on their approachability, the Abbasid rulers generally held themselves to be above day-to-day contact with the populace. Gaining access to the caliph was, at best, a tortuous affair, involving contact with a whole host of courtiers and officials who guarded their ruler's privacy with considerable zeal: after all, one mistake could bring into action the hooded executioner – the prime symbol of the Abbasid caliphate – who always stood next to the caliph, his sword at the ready.

The construction of Baghdad, with the caliph as both the physical and symbolic heart of the city, embodied the centralization of absolute power in the hands of one individual like never before. The Abbasid dynasty was now more powerful than its founder could ever have dreamed. Furthermore, al-Mansur's son, al-Mahdi, sought during his brief reign (775–85) to build bridges between the various religious factions of the day, and was thus able to provide the caliphate with arguably the only thing it lacked: a degree of orthodox religious support.

After the short reign of his eldest son, al-Hadi, the pious al-Mahdi was succeeded by his younger son, the legendary Harun al-Rashid. If ever the fabulous world of the *1001 Nights* had a real-life simulacrum, then it was to be found in the opulence and splendour of court life under Harun, whose reign (786–809) is often seen as the pinnacle of Abbasid prosperity and cultural brilliance. However, others – especially the more religiously minded of the Muslim historians – see this as a period more of excess than success, citing Harun's open flaunting of Islamic mores as the first nail in the Abbasid coffin, and, as such, as a portent of the eventual decay of the caliphal edifice. True, Harun was known publicly to be a wine-drinker and fornicator, whose penchant for the pleasures of the flesh was mirrored in the verse of his favourite court poet, Abu Nuwas (d. 803). The poetry of Abu Nuwas, celebrating the joys of wine, music and prepubescent boys, did nothing to endear the poet and his patron to the Muslim scholars, the *ulama*,[4] most of whom were careful to avoid being linked in any way to the caliph or his court.

Nevertheless, both Harun and his son, al-Ma'mun (813–33), were, like their predecessors, open supporters of the *shari'a* and did much during their reigns to further the cause of Islamic learning. This period of Abbasid rule is, thanks in no small way to court patronage, notable for the advances made in all of the Islamic disciplines. Sunni *fiqh*, or jurisprudence, reached maturity with the evolution of distinct 'schools of law' or 'rites' (*madhhab*) in various geographical centres. The emergence of the Iraqi school of *fiqh* under Abu Hanifa (d. 767) led eventually to the emergence of the Hanafi rite, to which over a third of Muslims still adhere. This was followed by the Medinan or Maliki school of law, developed out of the work of Malik b. Anas (d. 795); the Shafi'ite school, based on the teachings of Muhammad b. Idris al-Shafi'i (d. 820); and the Hanbali school, named after the Baghdad scholar Ahmad b. Hanbal (d. 855).

The codification of Islamic jurisprudence would not have been possible, of course, without the development of the 'science of *hadith*', which was underway at this time. Study of the Prophet's sayings or 'Traditions', and scholarly research into their authenticity and 'chains of transmission', had begun very early on, but it was not until the ninth century that the first major collections of *hadith* began to appear. In Sunni Islam, the most famous collections are known as the 'Six Books'; of these, the works of Bukhari (d. 870) and Muslim (d. 875) are considered the most authoritative – to the extent, in fact, that they are accorded a status second only to that of the Koran itself. The 'Six Books', together with the Koran, form the 'sources of law' in Sunni Islam, from which legal rulings are derived. The study of *hadith* was also cultivated by the Shi'ites, albeit slightly later. However, the Shi'ites have 'Four Books', and rely not only on the Traditions of the Prophet but also on the sayings of the twelve Imams.

The discipline of *kalam*, or scholastic theology, also began to emerge in the early Abbasid period, dealing with issues such as the nature of God and His attributes, the 'created' or 'uncreated' nature of the Koran, and the issue of free will and predestination. Foremost among the various theological 'schools' were the Mu'tazilites, the so-called rationalists of classical Islam, who championed the use of reason in all matters theological and philosophical; and their adversaries, the Ash'arites, for whom reason must always be informed by revelation. The Mu'tazilite approach was popular in many circles until the eleventh century, when the Ash'arite stance took over, later becoming the basis for all Sunni theology. So strong had the traditionalist position become by the end of the eleventh century that the Sunni *ulama* were able to declare the 'gate of *ijtihad*' – the use of independent reasoning to derive legal rulings – closed. Shi'ite theology developed along different lines and was used mostly to prove the authority and infallibility of the Twelve Imams of the house of Ali. Influenced to an extent by Mu'tazilite teachings, the Shi'ite *ulama* continued to promote the use of reason in law and theology, and for them the 'gate of *ijtihad*' remained open.

Parallel to developments in the sphere of mainstream Islamic learning was the growth of Sufism, which had appeared as early as the first century of Islam. Sufism – or, as some have termed it, Islamic mysticism – developed out of the assertion made by some that to live by God's laws was not enough: while the *shari'a* had always provided an exterior path of law to which one must submit in order to please God, it did not satisfy the innate desire of the human heart to enter directly into communion with God, and in doing so to know, love and worship Him as had so obviously been required of mankind in the Koran. The legalistic religion of the *ulama*, it was claimed, did not cater for this very human need, and thus it was to compensate for the deficiencies of orthodox religion that the movement known as Sufism came into existence. The term *Sufi* was coined in the ninth century, possibly as a name for those mystics whose ascetic practices and devotions included the donning of garments made out of *suf*, or coarse wool. By the time of Harun al-Rashid, the term referred to the generality of Muslim mystics, whether they engaged in ascetic practices or not. By the ninth century, the Sufis had begun to teach and write about the methods which, they claimed, could lead to the gnostic knowledge of God. The archetypal Sufi, described as a traveller (*salik*) on a journey, follows a path of seven stages: repentance; abstinence; renunciation; poverty; patience; trust in God; and complete submission to God's will. At the end of this path, the mystic traveller attains, with God's grace, a higher level of awareness which enables him to see, through the eye of the heart, that knowledge, the knower and the thing known are, in one respect, all one. While approaches and methodologies varied from Sufi to Sufi, the underlying message – namely that man was created in order to know himself, and, in knowing himself, to know God – was the same, and, they claimed, it was only through the Sufi path that such knowledge was attainable. Throughout the ninth and tenth centuries, Sufism grew throughout the Muslim world; famous mystics such as al-Muhasibi (d. 857) and Junayd (d. 910), both of Baghdad, and Persian gnostics such as Abu Yazid al-Bistami (d. 874) and the notorious Mansur al-Hallaj (d. 922) all made important contributions to the development of Sufi thought.

Under Ma'mun, we also see the beginnings of Islamic philosophy. Sympathetic to Mu'tazilite rationalism, Ma'mun built a vast library and institute of research known as the '*bayt al-hikma*', or 'House of Wisdom', which he stocked with manuscripts on philosophy, medicine, astronomy, astrology, mathematics and the natural sciences, brought from various parts of the old Byzantine and Sassanid empires by Christian and Jewish scholars. These manuscripts were then rendered into Arabic, thus acquainting the Muslim scholars with the works of Plato and Aristotle, Euclid and Galen. Known as the 'translation movement', this endeavour not only facilitated the growth of an indigenous Islamic philosophy, based initially on the teachings of Aristotle, but also served as a conduit through which classical learning, via translation from Arabic to Latin, would pass back into Europe centuries later, thus forming, as some Muslims claim, one of the bases for the Renaissance.

Ma'mun's successor, al-Mu'tasim (r. 833–42), moved the capital from Baghdad to a newly constructed city on the Tigris, Samarra. But a change of scenery could not mask the fact that the Abbasids were in trouble: the Turkish soldiers employed by Harun al-Rashid to protect the caliphate had now started to turn against it, and by the end of al-Mu'tasim's reign, they were virtually ruling in all but name. Their power grew even greater under al-Wathiq (r. 842), whom they eventually murdered. The Abbasid star was on the wane.

MUSLIM SPAIN

Paradoxically, as the Abbasids began to decline, an earlier offshoot of the Baghdad caliphate had taken root in southern Spain, and was now thriving. By the end of the seventh century, the Arabs had already established a strong presence in North Africa, having founded the garrison town of Qairawan, in modern-day Tunisia, as early as 667. From there, the Arabs conquered the rest of the Maghrib and, in 711, crossed the water to Spain; the word Gibraltar – the first Muslim foothold in Europe – is derived from the Arabic *jabal Tariq* ('Tariq's mountain'), named in honour of the commander of the Arab forces, Tariq b. Ziyad. The mixture of Arab and Berber forces behind Tariq were soon joined by a new wave of Arabs from the east, and before long the conquest of Spain was under way. Apart from the north-west, which remained Christian, most of the peninsula was under Muslim control within four years. The rate of Muslim expansion through Spain was breathtaking. Indeed, the move north would have continued into France, too, had it not been checked by Charles Martel (d. 741) at the battle of Poitiers in 732. Had the Muslims been victorious, the religious map of Europe – and with it possibly the history of the Western world – might have been very different.

After 717 the territories captured by the Muslim Arabs were governed by a succession of emirs, appointed by the caliphs in Damascus. However, in-fighting among the various governors and commanders led to misrule and disorder, with the appointment and deposition of no fewer than twenty emirs in forty years. This state of affairs came to an end with the arrival in Andalusia of 'Abd al-Rahman, grandson of the caliph Hisham. During the Abbasid revolution, while most members of the Umayyad ruling house were being slaughtered, 'Abd al-Rahman managed to escape across North Africa to Spain. There he defused the power struggle between the emirs and, in 756, established himself – in name of the Umayyads – as sole ruler of Andalusia (r. 756–88). This marked the first instance of regional separation from the Abbasid caliphate in Baghdad.

Under 'Abd al-Rahman's successors, the Umayyad emirate went from strength to strength, culturally as well as politically. The stability which obtained under 'Abd al-Rahman II (822–52) allowed for an efflorescence of art, culture and commerce. The great Mosque of Cordoba, begun by 'Abd al-Rahman I, was enlarged, and religious scholarship, spearheaded by *ulama* from the Maliki school of law, was patronized.

However, Andalusian civilization reached its zenith under 'Abd al-Rahman III (r. 912–61), whose political self-assurance was such that he was able to declare himself caliph in 921, thus breaking away from Baghdad once and for all. Under him, the capital – Cordoba – was transformed into possibly the most splendid city in the western world. Like his predecessors, 'Abd al-Rahman III was a great lover of the arts; he himself was a poet and author of some talent. He also fostered the spread of education and learning: numerous schools were built, in which the poor were often taught for free, and in the religious seminaries a whole new generation of Andalusian scholars emerged, versed in disciplines such as medicine, mathematics, philosophy and theology.

The peace and prosperity enjoyed by Umayyad Spain under 'Abd al-Rahman III contrasts sharply with the political instability and social disruption which beset the reigns of his successors, foreshadowing the eventual disintegration of Muslim rule in the peninsula. From the beginning of the eleventh century onwards, the Cordoba caliphate splintered into a number of petty emirates and kingdoms, led by power-hungry dynasts – the so-called 'faction kings'. This was a period of political intrigue, in-fighting, lawlessness and bloodshed, and the ensuing disunity among the various Muslim kings and emirs was exploited to full effect by the Christian kings of the north, to whom the 'faction kings' were forced to pay tribute. Consequently, in an attempt to regain control over their former territories, the Christian rulers of northern Spain were able to move southwards, meeting little resistance. Toledo fell in 1085, followed in 1094 by Valencia, which was recaptured by the famous El Cid – whose name derives from the Arabic *sayyidi*, 'my lord', and whose legendary exploits were chronicled in a rather one-sided Hollywood film of the same name.

By the end of the eleventh century, the progress of the Christian *reconquista* appeared inexorable, and it was only the appearance of two new Islamic dynasties, both from North Africa, that stemmed the encroaching tide and bought time for the Muslims in Andalusia. The Almoravids (whose name derives, via Spanish, from the Arabic *al-murabitun*, meaning 'those who dwell in fortified monasteries') were a Berber dynasty who hailed from the deserts of southern Morocco. They had ruled independently over much of north-west Africa since 1056; three decades later, they crossed over into Spain, where they were able to put paid to the quarrelling 'faction kings' and restore a semblance of political stability. The Almoravids governed Andalusia from the Moroccan city of Marrakesh, which they had established as their capital in 1062.

The success of the Almoravid dynasty in Spain stemmed as much from the piety and austere spirituality of its leaders as from the innate strength and military prowess of the Berber warriors who championed its cause. Recognizing the authority of the Abbasid caliphs, in terms of rite and ritual the

Almoravids were staunch champions of the Sunni orthodoxy, insisting on the strict application of the *shari'a* while denouncing other interpretations of, and approaches to, Islam – such as Sufism or philosophy – as highly suspect; the books of Imam Ghazali, for instance, were publicly burnt, and the use of reason in disciplines such as theology and Koranic exegesis was condemned as heretical.

However, the Almoravid dynasty became a victim of its own success sooner than most, falling prey to the corruption and dissipation that are often the lot of rulers who are given to unbridled excess. In 1118 they lost Zaragoza to Alfonso of Navarre and Aragon after a nine-month siege, and by 1145 they had left the peninsula altogether, thus allowing the Almohads, whose star was then waxing in North Africa, to become the new rulers of Islamic Spain.

The Almohads (from the Arabic *al-muwahhidun*, meaning 'those who affirm the Divine Unity') were also Berber in origin, evolving from the followers of Ibn Tumart (1080–1130), a self-proclaimed *mahdi* – the chiliastic figure who, it is believed, will reappear at the end of time – and religious reformer in the vein of Imam Ghazali. His successor, 'Abd al-Mu'min, conquered Morocco and established himself as ruler in Marrakesh in 1147. From there, the Almohads looked towards Spain, marching into Andalusia in 1160 with an army of a quarter of a million men. Within less than a decade, most of southern Spain was theirs. However, like their predecessors, the Almohads did not rule for long, and by 1250 their power in the region was dwindling.

The last Muslim stronghold in Spain belonged to the Nasirid dynasty, which ruled over the small kingdom of Granada from

1231 to 1492. The Christians, under Fernando II of Castile, had reconquered Cordoba in 1236 and Seville in 1248 – aided on both occasions by the eponymous founder of the Nasirid kingdom, Muhammad b. Yusuf b. Ahmed b. Nasir b. al-Ahmar – but while it appeared that the whole of the Iberian peninsula would fall once more into Christian hands, Granada was able to remain Muslim for another 250 years. The watershed came towards the end of the fifteenth century with the marriage of Ferdinand of Aragon to Isabella of Castile and León: their alliance united Spain and strengthened the Christian cause beyond estimation. Following the fall of Granada on 2 January 1492, which marked the end of seven hundred years of Islamic civilization in Spain, many Muslims left the peninsula and embarked on new lives elsewhere, mostly in North Africa; those who remained were subjected to considerable hardship and oppression at the hands of their new Christian masters. It was Ferdinand and Isabella's wish that all traces of Islamic culture be extirpated from Spanish society, and such suppression continued until the expulsion from Spain of the last remaining Muslims in the middle of the seventeenth century.

THE DECLINE OF THE CALIPHATE

Meanwhile, back in Baghdad, the growing influence of the Turkish mercenaries and the inability of the ruling elite to create an effective governmental apparatus independent of the caliph meant that by the end of the ninth century, the Abbasids were little more than puppet rulers. Although the caliphate was to limp on for another three hundred years, real power belonged to the semi-autonomous provincial governors, who were allowed to collect taxes and raise armies to maintain law and order in their own names. Gradually, as Abbasid power declined throughout the empire, numerous new dynasties sprang up, some paying lip-service to the caliph, others claiming independence.

One of the first regional dynasties to emerge was that of the Samanids, who ruled in eastern Iran from 819 to 1005. It was during the Samanid era that a new form of Persian language appeared, based on the ancient Pahlavi but enhanced by a large number of Arabic loan words. The new language formed the basis for the renaissance of Persian literature which occurred at this time, championed by figures such as Ferdowsi – Iran's national poet – and Rudaki, and patronized by the Samanid rulers from their twin capitals of Samarkand and Bukhara. The efflorescence of Persian culture during this period was so far-reaching that it effectively broke the monopoly hitherto enjoyed by the Arabic language over Islamic civilization. The Samanids later lost control of their lands to the Ghaznavids, a dynasty founded by Sebuktegin, son of a Turkish slave of the Samanids who had attained to a position of great influence in Samanid government circles. The Ghaznavids were also patrons of the arts, and it was to the Ghaznavid court at Ghazni, in the Afghan mountains, that Ferdowsi brought his epic poem *Shahnameh*, or 'Book of Kings'.

Elsewhere, dynasties were emerging apace. A branch of the Shi'ites known as Zaydis ruled the Caspian littoral independently from 864 to 928, while the Tulunids established a dynasty in Cairo at roughly the same time (868–906). In Tunisia, the Aghlabids ruled from 800–909, and later conquered Sicily, which they held until the end of the eleventh century. The Aghlabids were replaced in North Africa by the Fatimids, another Shi'ite offshoot, who ruled from 909 to 972. The dynasty, which came to prominence through its leadership of the Ismaili movement,[5] occupied Egypt in 969, whereupon its rulers assumed the titles of both imam and caliph. The Fatimids were later replaced by the Ayyubid dynasty, founded by the legendary Kurdish military leader, Saladin (d. 1193). The Ayyubids failed to survive as a dynasty more than sixty years after their founder's death, and the petty squabbles between those who considered themselves his heirs opened the way for the Mamluks, a dynasty formed from slave soldiers of the Ayyubid army.

Meanwhile, as puppets of the Turkish mercenaries, the Abbasid caliphs were floundering. Of the twelve caliphs who followed Mutawakkil (d. 861), six were murdered, the other six imprisoned or blinded. To rescue the Abbasid state from these appalling conditions, the caliph al-Mustaqfi (r. 944–6) invited a family of military leaders, the Buyids, to take control of Baghdad. This they did in 945, assuming the old Persian title of *shahanshah*, or 'king of kings'. The Buyids were Shi'ites, a fact which gave rise to the anomaly of an Abbasid caliph being forced to surrender temporal power to a heterodox sect while himself having to be content with what amounted to little more than the empty prestige of the caliphal title. The Buyids were able to restore a modicum of peace and stability to the ailing regime, simultaneously overseeing great advances in scholarship and the arts; but the revival was short lived. Eventually, they declined into a group of squabbling, power-hungry princelings, and were ousted with alacrity by yet another Turkish dynasty, the Seljuks.

The Seljuks, who had defeated the Ghaznavids in 1030 and divided up the conquered territories among their ruling families, captured Baghdad in 1055; within several decades they had succeeded in reuniting much of the eastern wing of the Islamic world and, under the authority of the Abbasids, recovering areas which had been appropriated by local rulers and the Fatimids, including Syria and Palestine.

Yet the Seljuks did not consider themselves to be caliphs. The official title of the Seljuk ruler was *sultan*, or 'holder of authority', a new term in Muslim political vocabulary which was used to denote the actual holder of power in society, as distinct from the *khalifa*. The sultanate system of the Seljuks was based largely upon Persian bureaucracy, with the well-known vizier Nizam al-Mulk as its lynchpin. Nizam al-Mulk's major contribution to Islamic civilization was his founding of the first university in the Muslim world, the famous Nizamiyyeh school or *madrasa*, which was established in 1066; a network of similar institutions later sprang up in most of the major cities of the land. These schools fostered the theology of al-Ash'ari and trained generations of *ulama* in the disciplines of hadith and Islamic law.

One outstanding product of the *madrasa* system was al-Ghazali (d. 1111), possibly medieval Islam's greatest scholar. Born in 1058 at Tus in eastern Persia, he was made head of the Baghdad *nizamiyyeh* in 1091. For four years, to great acclaim, he taught both law and jurisprudence and produced stinging critiques of philosophy and Ismaili doctrine. However, he later wrote that the more he taught, the more sceptical he became, until finally he could teach no more. In 1095 he retired from public life and went into retreat with the aim of arriving at a more satisfying understanding of Islam. When he emerged, ten years later, he brought with him a system of ideas that combined the introspective religion of the mystics with the exoteric practices of mainstream Islam, thus reconciling Sufism with Sunni orthodoxy once and for all. For his pains he was acknowledged as a 'renewer' (*mujaddid*), a role expected by most Muslims to be filled by at least one scholar at the turn of every century.

After Nizam al-Mulk's death in 1092 at the hands of an Ismaili 'assassin', the Seljuk empire fractured into a number of independent principalities,[6] thus robbing the caliphate in Baghdad of the stability upon which its survival depended. When the end finally came for the Abbasids, with the Mongol destruction of their capital in 1258, it was far from merciful. Saunders describes the devastation wrought on Baghdad: 'The palace, college and mosques were plundered and burnt; the cultural accumulation of five centuries perished in the flames, and the appalling figure of 800,000 is the lowest estimate given of the number of men, women and children who were slaughtered in the streets and houses.'[7]

Before discussing the Mongol invasion, another threat to the world of Islam warrants consideration. Towards the end of the Abbasid period occurred a series of Christian–Muslim military encounters: the Crusades.

THE CRUSADES

The origin of the Crusades – a series of military enterprises conducted by western European Christians between 1095 and 1291 – is to be found in the upheaval caused by the expansion of the Seljuks through Anatolia and into Syria and Palestine in the middle of the eleventh century. Threatened by the new Turkish power, the Byzantines appealed to the Pope, Urban II, for military aid. In turn, Urban II appealed to the kings and princes of the Christian west for help, urging them to go forward under Christ's banner to wrest Jerusalem and other Palestinian places of pilgrimage – the 'Holy Land' – from Muslim control. The Pope may also have seen in this enterprise a means of diverting the rulers of Europe from their internecine struggles, as well as reuniting the western Church with that of the East.

Considered objectively, the enterprise was impossible. The volunteers – a disorganized and motley crew of kings, nobles and soldiers of fortune – had to march east, be ferried across the Bosphorus, then traverse thousands of miles of inhospitable terrain to face adversaries about whom they knew next to nothing. Yet the fervour to 'fight for Christ' was such that thousands flocked to the cause, although not all in the name of Christianity. For many, the idea of finding fortune in distant climes was just as important as, if not more so than, embracing martyrdom for the cause.

The idea that the enterprise was fuelled solely by sincere religious zeal on the part of the Christians is just one of the myths which surround the Crusades. Another is that of the 'chivalrous knight' pitted against the 'infidel Saracen', together with countless horror stories of Muslim atrocities carried out at the expense of helpless Christian communities in the Holy Land. Ideas and images such as these have long since been dispelled by objective historical studies of Muslim and Christian involvement in the Crusades, although the popular perception persists.

The stark difference in conduct between the Christian and Muslim forces in the first three Crusades is crystallized in the battle for Jerusalem, the city sacred to all three monotheistic faiths. Jerusalem had first fallen to the Muslims in 638, during the second caliph 'Umar's first wave of Islamic conquests; history records that the non-Muslim minorities of the city were subsequently treated with deference and compassion. By the mid-eleventh century, Jerusalem had become a wealthy cosmopolis, and although Seljuk domination of the former Byzantine territory had made it more difficult for Christian pilgrims to visit the Holy City, Jerusalem itself was still a shining example of mutual tolerance and understanding between adherents of the three resident faiths.

The First Crusade changed all of this. In July 1099 the Crusaders captured Jerusalem, where they were to establish a Christian kingdom that would last almost ninety years. In total contradistinction to the behaviour of their Muslim predecessors, the new Christian rulers did not treat the religious minorities under their control with the justice or respect owed to them as fellow believers in one God: a vast number of Muslims and Jews were massacred, including women and children. The Dome of the Rock was turned into a church, while al-Aqsa, one of the three most important places of Muslim worship, was converted into a royal palace for the new ruler, Godfrey of Bouillon. However, it was not only Jews and Muslims who were to bear the brunt of Christian brutality. Whereas under Muslim rule the Church of the Holy Sepulchre had been allowed to retain altars representing all of the eastern Christian sects, the crusading army strove to eradicate all rites and practices save for those of the Latin Church – a policy they attempted to effect by torturing the Orthodox priests.

The Crusaders also established principalities in Antioch, Tripoli, Tyre and Edessa, and it was the recapture of Edessa in 1144 by Zangi, the Muslim governor of Mosul, that precipitated the Second Crusade. Proclaimed by Pope Eugenius III and led by Louis VII of France and Conrad III of Germany, the Second Crusade began with disastrous campaigns in Anatolia and Syria, and culminated in ignominy when the Crusaders failed in their attempt to besiege Damascus, thanks mainly to lack of support from the Byzantine emperor, Manuel.

Of all the Crusades it in perhaps the Third (1189–92) which has the most resonance for Muslims, for it brought to prominence and world renown one of their greatest military heroes. Born in Mesopotamia, Salah al-Din Yusuf ibn Ayyub – known to the rest of the world as Saladin – entered the service of the Zangids and, on the death of their leader, Nur al-Din (1174), proclaimed himself *sultan* of Syria. From there he reduced Mesopotamia and received the homage of the Seljuk princes of Anatolia. His later years were spent in battle with the Christians, and it was defeat of the field army of the Latin Kingdom of Jerusalem at Hittin in July 1187 that precipitated the Third Crusade. Led by three of the greatest rulers of Christendom, Frederick I ('Barbarossa') of Germany, Philip II of France and Richard I ('the Lionheart') of England, the Crusade promised much but achieved little. Frederick I drowned in an Anatolian river before he had even arrived, while the thinly veiled hostility between the French and the English was hardly conducive to an effective campaign. The only positive outcome for the Christian forces was the five-year peace treaty concluded between the Lionheart and Saladin, guaranteeing pilgrims access to the Holy Places.

The Fourth Crusade (1202–4), proclaimed by Pope Innocent IV, was launched with the aim of attacking the Muslims of Egypt and recapturing the Holy Places in Palestine. However, beset by financial problems, the Crusaders were unable to pay the Venetians for their ships, and were therefore diverted from their original objective and forced instead into supporting the Venetian attempt to capture Constantinople, which fell to them in 1204. Under the pretext of restoring Isaac II and his son Alexius to their former position of power in Byzantium, the city was sacked and pillaged, and, notwithstanding the fact that the Byzantine empire survived for another two centuries, it never really recovered from the blow. A Latin empire was established and Godfrey of Bouillon's brother, Baldwin of Flanders, was installed as the first Latin emperor of Constantinople. This episode damaged beyond repair the little credibility that the concept of the Crusades had in the eyes of the Eastern Orthodoxy, and destroyed any possibility of future co-operation between the Eastern and Western Churches. Not only did intra-Christian relations worsen as a result, but also the original objectives of Pope Innocent IV were not addressed at all.

The later Crusades were directed mostly against North Africa, the received wisdom being that the only way to secure Palestine was by eradicating the Ayyubids (and later the Mamluks) from Egypt. In 1219 the Fifth Crusade, led by the combined forces of France and Germany, succeeded in taking the town of Damietta, whereupon an eight-year truce was agreed. Ten years later the leader of the Sixth Crusade, Emperor Frederick II, crowned himself king of Jerusalem as part of treaty which stipulated that Jerusalem return to Christian control for ten years. King Louis IX of France led the Seventh Crusade to Egypt in 1248 and the Eighth Crusade, also to North Africa, in 1270. This latter Crusade did have some success in that it gave rise to the negotiation of a truce between the future King Edward I of England and the Mamluks, and the negotiation of a treaty between Charles of Anjou, king of Naples and Sicily, and Tunis.

All in all, these later Crusades were, despite their professed aims, nothing more than a series of intra-Christian wars – campaigns sanctioned by the Pope ostensibly to curtail the 'Saracen threat', while in reality serving as papal wars against those Christians deemed heretical. Of these later enterprises, only the aforementioned Sixth Crusade made any considerable impact on the Holy Land itself, and then solely to the detriment of the Crusaders themselves: the treaty negotiated by Emperor Frederick II, under the terms of which the Ayyubids would cede to his rule, was signed while the emperor was still under excommunication by the Pope. This in effect meant that as far as the papacy itself was concerned, Frederick's recapture of Jerusalem did not count, thus serving to emphasize exactly how futile much of the Crusading enterprise had been. Fifteen years later, Jerusalem returned to Muslim control when the Latin invaders were defeated by a largely Egyptian army, while it was down to the Mamluks to drive the Latins out of the Holy Land for good at the end of the thirteenth century.

The Crusades had been launched with apparent aim of saving the lands of eastern Christendom from the warriors of Islam, but by the time they ended in 1291, most of the territory in question was firmly under Muslim control. Rather than strengthening Christendom, the Crusades had weakened it beyond repair; rather than uniting all Christians in the face of their Muslim foes, the Crusaders had done more or less the opposite. One of the most serious consequences of the whole enterprise was the deleterious effect it had on Christian minorities in the Holy Land. As one historian asserts, 'formerly these minorities had been accorded rights and privileges under Muslim rule, but after the establishment of the Latin Kingdom, they found themselves treated as "loathsome schismatics"'. In an effort to obtain relief from their fellow Christians, many abandoned their Nestorian or Monophysite beliefs, and adopted either Roman Catholicism, or – the supreme irony – Islam.'[8]

Yet the eventual outcome of the Crusades was in many ways a positive one for both sides. When hostilities ceased, various trade routes opened up between the cities of Europe and those in the Muslim world. Trade brought increased contact between the two cultures, each of which was eager to borrow from the other. Arguably, the West had the better deal, obtaining many new ideas and material possessions from a civilization that was considerably more advanced than its own. Western merchants found themselves trading in items hitherto unknown in Europe, such as sugar, maize, lemons, melons, rice, cotton cloth, spices and perfumes. Thanks to knowledge gained from the study of Arab works, advances were made in science, medicine, art and architecture. Features of everyday life we now take for granted, such as glass mirrors, clocks, paper and carpets, began to appear in western homes, along with Arabic numerals and a whole host of Arabic words. Most important of all, however, was the strategic significance of the opening up of sea trade routes. As we shall see later, control of the eastern trade became a constantly recurring theme in later relations between Europe and the Muslim world, and would lead, several centuries later, to a considerably more successful form of western intervention in Muslim affairs than the Crusaders could ever have imagined.

THE MONGOL INVASION

As far as most Muslims are concerned, the episode of the Crusades represents no more than a minute tear in the fabric of their history. The Mongol invasion, however, is a different matter: not only did it rend that fabric apart, it also threatened to consume it entirely. The impact of the invasion was immeasurable, and not without a certain amount of justification have some Muslim historians spoken of this disaster as being tantamount to Islam's own holocaust. The Mongols emerged like a whirlwind out of the semi-barren steppes of central Asia and, within decades, went on to terrorize several civilizations, plundering, pillaging and slaughtering on a scale surpassed only by the technologically aided wars of our own century, before disappearing almost as rapidly as they had come.

United under the fearsome Genghis Khan in 1206, the confederation of nomadic tribes known as the Mongols had become masters of northern China by 1217. From China they moved westwards, destroying everything in their path. A year later they attacked the powerful empire of Khwarizm before moving on to Samarkand and Bukhara, which they captured in 1220, returning home five years later. Meanwhile, two of Genghis's lieutenants moved northwards from the Caspian littoral into southern Russia and the Crimea, returning by way of the Volga, but not before laying waste to every city they encountered.

By 1255 most of central Asia was under the control of Hulagu, Genghis's grandson. For the Muslims, however, the psychological watershed was the fall of Baghdad in 1258, which finally brought an end to what was left of the Abbasid empire, and with it the institution of the caliphate itself. Legend has it that the last Abbasid ruler, al-Musta'sim, was rolled up in one of his own carpets and trampled to death. The rest of the Muslim world resisted the Mongol advances at its peril. Within two years of the fall of Baghdad, most of the Muslim world, apart from Arabia, Syria, Egypt and North Africa, had been overrun. In 1260, Hulagu moved against Palestine and Egypt, and had it not been for the death of the Great Khan, Mongke, he might have secured success there too. However, news of his leader's demise sent him and many of his forces marching back to China, leaving only a fraction of his army for the Mamluks of Egypt to defeat.

Clearly the enormity of the Mongol onslaught is not to be underestimated. The one aspect of this tragic episode which galls Muslims most is the fact that the Mongols seemed to take delight in killing for its own sake: simple conquest, rather than the promise of booty or the attraction of settlement, appeared to propel them forward. All bloodshed, it can be argued, is ultimately devoid of reason, but the first wave of Mongol depredations must surely have seemed more devoid of reason than most, even to those who were used to the often bloody changeover of regimes. In a great swathe from Samarkand to Baghdad, the Mongols visited death and destruction upon community after community, slaughtering the populations of whole cities to a man, their only calling-card the hideous towers of skulls that they are said to have left behind. Libraries, schools and other repositories of learning would be destroyed, while mosques, monuments and palaces would be razed to the ground: it is said that in some towns, the extent of Mongol ferocity was such that nothing but ashes were left, and within years it was as though no building had ever stood or plant grown or living thing breathed and moved there, since time began.

For a while, Muslims under Mongol rule found themselves governed from Peking, although by 1258 they were divided between three vast Mongol states: the Chagatai Mongols of central Asia; the Golden Horde in the Volga Basin; and the Il-Khanate of Iran and Iraq. Hulagu was the first to style himself 'Il-Khan'; his successors, the Ilkhanids, were to dominate Iran for another hundred years. However, the Ilkhanids differed from their Mongol forefathers in that they adopted Islam and became Persianized.

For all its vicissitudes, the Ilkhanid period remains, paradoxically, one of the most brilliant in Iranian history. The Ilkhanids were renowned patrons of all branches of Islamic learning, and the arts and sciences flourished as never before. Nasir al-Din Tusi, both astronomer and philosopher, built an observatory at Maragheh in modern-day Iran, the first observatory – in the modern sense of the word – in the history of science. He also developed the mathematical calculations showing the earth's spherical shape and size and its movement around the sun, thus predating the work of Copernicus by some two hundred years. No less a scientist was the famed Ulugh Beg, who also wrote many seminal treatises on various aspects of astronomy, while in the field of optics, Kamal al-Din Farsi made major advances with his theories on refraction and reflection. In Tabriz, Rashid al-Din, the world historian, was at his peak, while in the Samarkand of the Ilkhanids, Sa'd al-Din Taftazani was penning works of philosophy that have remained at the core of Islamic learning up until the present day. Miniature painting, demonstrating distinct Chinese influences, flourished and took on a distinctly Islamic colouring, while new forms of architecture were developed in earnest by Ilkhanid rulers, who were only too eager to rebuild what their forefathers had destroyed.

The overall result was that Persian culture was developed and spread to such an extent that it became the most outstanding in the Islamic world. Nowhere is this more apparent than in the world of belles-lettres. In the field of literature in general, and poetry in particular, the Mongol-Ilkhanid period remains the most fruitful in the history of Iran, and arguably in the history of Islam itself. At the beginning of the Mongol era, Sa'adi (1213–92) wrote two of the Persian language's most significant works, *Bustan* and *Golestan*. Emphasizing the salvific love of God and the interdependence of all mankind regardless of nationality, race

or religion, his poetry wooed audiences not only in his native
Persia but also in places as far afield as India, central Asia and
China. In the following century, Hafez (1320–90), a Sufi and
arguably the greatest lyric poet of the Persian language, wrote
his immortal *Divan*, a work characterized by the author's sense
of beauty, love of humanity and devotion to God. That Sa'adi
and Hafez vie with Ferdowsi for the title of Iran's national poet
is testimony both to their worth and to the embarrassment of
riches that was Persian poetry offered during this period.

The Mongol spectre was resurrected briefly by the appearance,
at the end of the fourteenth century, of another warrior from
the East, Taymur-i Lang ('Taymur the lame'), or 'Tamburlaine',
as he was immortalized by Christopher Marlowe. Although not
a direct descendant of Genghis Khan, Taymur certainly came
from the same barbaric tradition. Having ascended the throne
of Samarkand in 1369, he embarked on a series of conquests
that were every bit as devastating as those of his Mongol
predecessors. He conquered Persia (1392–6), Georgia and the
Tatar empire, before moving south to capture all of the
territories between the Indus and the lower Ganges (1398).
Later, he won Damascus and Syria from the Egyptian Mamluks
and defeated the Ottomans at Ankara. He died while marching
to conquer China. The dynastic group descended from him,
the Timurids, went on to rule Persia and parts of central Asia
after his death. Fortunately for the Persians, the Timurid forte
was not for bloodshed but for learning and the arts. The
sultanate of Husayn Bayqara (r. 1470–1506), who filled his
court with poets, painters and architects, is usually seen as the
high point of Timurid Islamic culture.

THREE

The Medieval Era

THE OTTOMAN EMPIRE

As one dynasty of Turks – the Seljuks of Baghdad and Rum – was being overwhelmed by the Mongol invasion, another Turkish dynasty – the Ottomans – was beginning to make its mark. Osman (1259–1326), its eponymous founder, began his career as leader of a minor nomadic tribe in eastern Anatolia; by the end of his career, he had subdued a considerable area of Asia Minor.

The notion that the Ottomans would prove to be just another in a long line of lawless Turkish warrior nomads was dispelled early on by Osman's son, Orhan (r. 1324–60), under whose reign there began a process of state building and settlement of conquered territories that was to underpin Ottoman military might and ensure the dynasty's longevity. The first move towards the creation of a new empire came in 1326, when Orhan captured the city of Bursa and made it his capital. Subsequently, he styled himself *sultan* – the first of his dynasty to do so – and issued the first Ottoman coinage.

Expansion westwards continued, gaining momentum during the reign of Orhan's son, Murad I (r. 1360–89), who is recognized as being the first of the Ottoman rulers to lead

Ottoman forces into Europe proper. Under Murad's leadership, Thrace was conquered and raids were made into western Bulgaria. In 1366, the city of Edirne (Adrianople) was established as the Ottomans' European capital. From there they were in a position to fend off Serbian advances and, as a result, occupy most of Macedonia. In the mid-1380s Sofia and Nis were captured, thus providing the Ottomans with a firm foothold in the Balkans. The culmination of Murad's European adventures came with the battle of Kosovo in 1389, in which Murad's forces gained a famous victory over the Serbs and he himself was killed. Murad's reign was important insofar as it marked the transition of the role of the Ottoman ruler from being simply one of a group of warring nomad leaders to being the *sultan* of territories whose size and importance required the kind of statecraft hitherto thought beyond the ken and competence of the minor Anatolian dynasts.

Under Murad's son, Bayezid I (r. 1389–1402), Ottoman expansion continued apace, and within three years he had conquered the rest of Bulgaria and parts of Serbia, Macedonia and Thessaly. Not unjustifiably, then, did the rapidity of his conquests earn him the nickname *Yildirim*, or 'Lightning'. However, Bayezid broke the unwritten rule which deemed that Ottoman expansion should take place at the expense of the ailing Christian states alone: storming through Anatolia, he began to conquer the Turkish principalities in the east – lands which had traditionally been acquired through marriage or purchase, not by brute force. In 1402 Bayezid was captured by Taymur during the latter's brief invasion of Anatolia, only to die in prison a year later. The empire was later restored by his son, Mehmed I (r. 1413–21), and enhanced by Murad II (r. 1421–44), who revived Ottoman fortunes in Europe as far as the Danube; in the process, he rooted out the various Christian rulers of Serbia and Bulgaria and replaced them with Ottoman officials and administrators.

Murad II's policy was continued by the man whom many call the real founder of the Ottoman empire: Mehmed II (1432–81), also known as 'Mehmed The Conqueror' on account of his epic conquest of Constantinople in 1453, which he renamed Istanbul. Mehmed's capture of this vast city after a seven-week siege was the *coup de grace* which finally extinguished the Byzantine empire. From his commanding position on the Bosphorus, Mehmed was able to annex most of Serbia, all of Greece and most of the Greek islands; on the eastern front, he was able to subjugate Anatolia as far as the Euphrates.

As the Ottoman empire grew, so did the complexity of its institutions. One of the most important was the famous elite infantry corps known as the Janissaries (from the Turkish *yeni cheri*, or 'new force'). Established by Murad I, they were originally recruited from among prisoners of war; later, however, they were raised by a process known as *devshirme*, which was basically a levy from among the Christian subjects of the realm. Recruits were educated, converted to Islam and then given military training. Without the Janissaries, the expansion of the Ottoman empire would not have been possible. In addition to their military skills, the Ottomans came to command a superb talent for organization, presiding over a bureaucracy that was, in the early years, a model of administrative efficiency and discipline.

The Ottoman empire reached its zenith under the illustrious Sulayman (r. 1520–66), whose reign was of such brilliance that the Europeans were moved to add the title 'Magnificent' to his name. Under Sulayman the Magnificent, the Ottoman territories inherited from his father were doubled, thus bringing into existence a multicultural, multilingual, multifaith empire which stretched from Vienna in the west to the fringes of the Arabian peninsula in the east, and from the Black Sea in the north to the deserts of lower Egypt in the south. Yet the man to whose name his countrymen added the epithet 'the Lawgiver' on account of the system of laws he introduced to regulate land tenure was not merely a military strategist. Under Sulayman, the Ottoman empire witnessed an unprecedented flowering of art and architecture, with the *sultan* as their staunchest patron. Bridges, public baths, religious seminaries and mosques were built, including the magnificent Sülemaniye Mosque complex in Istanbul and the Selimiye Mosque in Edirne, both constructed by the incomparable master architect Mimar Sinan (1489–1588). The fine arts also flourished, with miniature painting enjoying considerable growth and popularity. Sulayman's reign is also deemed to be the golden age of Ottoman verse, with the *sultan* himself ranking among the most accomplished poets of the day. And in the religious sciences, both theology and law flourished as never before.

While Sulayman was helping to reconstruct the greatest power in the eastern Mediterranean since the golden age of Byzantium, momentous changes were under way on the empire's eastern front. It is to Persia and the rise of the Safavid dynasty that we now turn.

THE BIRTH OF THE IRANIAN STATE AND
THE RISE OF TWELVER SHI'ISM

Fifteenth-century Iran was dominated by two religious currents: extremist folk-Sufism, or *ghuluww*, with its highly unorthodox and even heretical beliefs and markedly pro-Shi'ite tendencies; and mainstream or 'high' Sufism, epitomized by orthodox Sunni brotherhoods such as the Mawlawiyya (the forerunners of the Mevlevi 'whirling' dervishes), the Ni'matullahiyya and the Naqshbandiyya. Unlike the 'high' Sufis, the *ghulat*, or extremists, seemed largely to have considered the *shari'a* defunct, and its laws and ordinances went unheeded. Undisciplined religiosity allowed political and military ambition to run riot, and it is largely from the *ghulat* that the various popular anti-establishment revolts which took place in eastern Anatolia and Iran proper during this period found their inspiration.

In matters of religious law, the majority of the Iranian populace was Sunni, adhering to the Shafi'ite and Hanafite schools of jurisprudence. The rise of Sufism in general, and *ghuluww* in particular, had gone hand-in-hand with a temporary decline in the fortunes of orthodox Islam, although the adherents of the high Sufi brotherhoods and other mystico-religious groups endeavoured to remain faithful to the letter of the law. Among these was the Safawiyya, or Safavid order, a Sunni Sufi brotherhood founded by Shaykh Safi of Ardabil (d. 1334). The Safavid order was highly respected by the political authorities both in Shaykh Safi's time and also during the leadership of his three immediate successors, Sadr al-Din (d. 1393), Khwaja 'Ali (d. 1429) and Shaykh Ibrahim (d. 1447); so popular and influential had the order become by the middle of the fifteenth century that its leaders were able to act as intermediaries between the political rulers of the day and their opponents.

With the succession of Shaykh Junayd (d. 1460), however, the order underwent a momentous transformation as the mainstream Sufism of Shaykh Safi was abandoned in favour of openly heterodox pro-Shi'ite extremism or *ghuluww*. The sudden religious *volte-face* was accompanied by a radical change in the order's political leanings, transforming it into a militant movement which, in less than half a century, grew in intensity and ambition to such a point that it was able to put Junayd's grandson, Ismail, on the throne as the first Safavid king of Persia.

This sudden change in religious orientation – from mainstream, Sunni Sufism to highly heterodox pro-Shi'ite extremism – should perhaps be seen in the light of the political change, and it must be concluded that the religious change was no more than a pretext for Shaykh Junayd's political aspirations. Junayd became leader of the Safavid order just months after the death of the last great Timurid ruler, Shahrukh (d. 1446). With the latter's demise, the political status quo in Iran and Transoxania was disrupted and the stage left open for the rival Aq-Qoyunlu ('White Sheep') and Qara-Qoyunlu ('Black Sheep') dynasties to vie for overall power. It was at this point that Junayd began to claim descent from the first Shi'ite Imam, Ali, asserting that his (Junayd's) descendants had more right to rule the Islamic community than even the companions of the Prophet. From Ardabil, the spiritual home of the Safavid order, Junayd travelled westwards among the unsettled Turkish tribes of rural Anatolia. They, with their history of anti-state militancy and their quasi-egalitarian, pro-Shi'ite religious extremism, would be ideal fighting material for the ambitious Junayd. Naturally, to win their allegiance he would have to forsake the quietistic Sufism of his forefathers and espouse the extremist cause: this, it is alleged, explains his claims to 'Alid descent. As Minorsky observes, 'it is possible that having discovered Shi'ite leanings among the Anatolians, he felt that a wider scope for his enterprise would open with his own move in the same direction.'[9] Junayd's aspiration for royal succession was enhanced by his marriage to the sister of Uzun Hasan, the Aq-Qoyunlu ruler. The Safavid leaders henceforth became known as 'princes of the land'. It was on the basis of this judiciously planned marriage that Junayd was able to exchange the epithet of *shaykh* for that of *sultan*.

Under the leadership of Junayd's son, Haydar (d. 1488), the Safavid order became crystallized as a political movement with an increasingly extremist religious colouring. So extreme had the order become, in fact, that Haydar was looked upon as divine by his followers, who became known as the Qizilbash ('red-heads') on account of the red twelve-pointed cap which Haydar instructed them to wear. Haydar had been installed in Ardabil in 1469 by his maternal uncle, Uzun Hasan, who had defeated the Qara-Qoyunlu dynasty and annexed its former domains. The return of the Safavid order to Ardabil prompted an influx of the movement's followers from eastern Anatolia and northern Syria, thus paving the way for the eventual Safavid conquest of Iran. This came in 1500, when Haydar's youngest son, Ismail, still only thirteen, led his Qizilbash supporters to a famous victory over the Aq-Qoyunlu

ruler of Azarbaijan. The following year, the Qizilbash entered
the Aq-Qoyunlu capital, Tabriz, where Ismail proclaimed
himself shah. By 1508, when Ismail succeeded in taking
Baghdad, the whole country was more or less under his
control.

Ismail's first act as ruler was to implement a religious policy
that has affected Iranian life ever since: he established Twelver
Shi'ism as the state religion. Given Ismail's spiritual allegiance
to the Twelve Imams, it was only logical that he and his
advisers would adopt a form of Islam that was not only in
keeping with their own pro-Shi'ite beliefs but which would also
serve to stabilize the state. Orthodox Twelver Shi'ism, with its
recognized set of principles and highly elaborate system of
dogma, was the natural choice; this despite the fact that Ismail
and his supporters were, like most of the Iranian people,
ignorant of the finer points of Twelver doctrine: the only
manual of Shi'ite jurisprudence to be found was one which
had long gathered dust in the corner of an obscure private
library, and historians of the time had trouble remembering
when Twelver Shi'ism had last played a role in Iran's affairs.
That Ismail's decision to impose Shi'ism was politically
motivated is certain, therefore. Twelver orthodoxy would have
the desired stabilizing effect, and its immediate propagation
was vital if the doctrinal uniformity so crucial to the Safavid
retention of power was to come about. Moreover, the adoption
of Shi'ism would effectively isolate Iran from her Sunni
neighbours and thus create a stronger sense of national
identity for the Safavids to exploit.

To carry out his policy, Ismail began to import Shi'ite
scholars from overseas. For three hundred years prior to the

advent of the Safavids, orthodox Twelver Shi'ism had developed mainly in small enclaves outside Iran, such as Jabal 'Amil in Lebanon, al-Ahsa and Bahrein. The first Twelver scholars imported by Ismail hailed from these areas, and from the outset it became clear that the doctrines they espoused were considerably different from those of the people upon whom they were to impose the new creed. As the immigrant Shi'ite scholars took up their new positions in Iran, they set about suppressing all forms of religious orientation other than their own. This was, of course, totally in line with the objectives of the nascent regime, for the consolidation of Safavid power depended on the ability of the new ruler to eradicate all potential centres of opposition. Sufism, Sunnism and Qizilbash extremism were all targets for the incoming Twelver jurists; vilification of the first three caliphs – Abu Bakr, 'Umar and Uthman – was institutionalized, and all those who objected to the new state of affairs were brutally silenced. Twelver scholars found convenient niches for themselves in the new administration, from which they were able to spread the traditions of the Twelve Imams and successfully impose their doctrines on the masses.

Shah Ismail died in 1524 and was succeeded by his ten-year-old son, Tahmasp (r. 1524–76). For the first decade of his reign, the young ruler was torn between his endeavours to prevent the Qizilbash from revolting and his attempts to keep the Uzbeks from taking Khorasan and the Ottomans from taking Tabriz. In 1533, while the Safavid army was busy fighting the Uzbeks on the eastern front, the Ottomans captured Baghdad, which they were to hold for a century. There then followed a series of Persian–Ottoman wars, concluded by

Treaty of Amasya (1555), which was to bring peace between the two nations for the next quarter of a century.

Under Shah Tahmasp, the influx of Twelver Shi'ite scholars from Lebanon and Bahrein continued unabated, and the Twelver *ulama* emerged as important players on the socio-religious stage in Safavid Iran. At the behest of the *ulama*, the shah ordered the closure of opium dens, taverns, gambling houses and brothels; members of his retinue were made to repent collectively; the jurists were ordered to 'enjoin the good and prohibit the bad' (*amr bi'l ma'ruf wa nahy 'an al-munkar*) from the pulpit; vast sums of money were donated to the holy shrines; wine cellars were emptied and bottles smashed in the street; and shaving was forbidden. If historians wish to locate the birth of Islamic 'fundamentalism' in Iran, they need look no further than the Iran of Shah Tahmasp.

Nevertheless, towards the end of Tahmasp's 52-year reign, the Safavid state began to turn away slightly from the strict theocracy imposed by Ismail and move towards a more secular administration. During the reign of Shah Ismail, both political and religious leadership had been vested in the personage of the shah, who was both ruler of Iran and head of the Safavid order. Tahmasp, aware of the need to play down the extremist origins of the dynasty in favour of the new orthodoxy, realized that the only way to do this would be to strip the monarchy of effective religious authority. To this end, he issued a decree (*farman*) which devolved upon the notorious Shaykh Karaki the responsibility of maintaining the *shari'a* as supreme religious authority of the realm; the shah was subsequently viewed in political terms, as a monarch, rather than as the head of the Safavid order. Yet while

Tahmasp's decree succeeded in separating state from religion and thus making his own temporal authority more acceptable, it also had the effect of creating a potentially dangerous rival power base. Tahmasp's decree is of immense historical significance, therefore, since it marks the beginning of the Twelver Shi'ite *ulama* as an autonomous centre of power, without which the Iranian revolution of 1979 would not have been possible.

Tahmasp was succeeded by his son, Ismail II, in 1576. Ismail II was renowned chiefly for his attempt to reinstate Sunnism as the official religion, appointing officials who were known for their Sunni sympathies and removing with no uncertain brutality anyone that dared to stand in his way. His policies outraged the fanatical Qizilbash, and it was probably one of their number who eventually took the matter into his own hands: a year after his accession, Ismail II was murdered as he lay sleeping with his young male lover.

After the ten-year rule of the ineffectual Shah Muhammad Khodabandeh (1577–87), the Safavid crown went to arguably the most politically astute and strategically brilliant member of the dynasty, the charismatic Shah 'Abbas I (r. 1587–1629). 'Abbas's task upon becoming shah was to revivify the ailing Safavid state, which with the death of Tahmasp had seemed near collapse. First, he turned his attention to military affairs, his objective being to win back the lands the earlier Safavids had lost. To this end, he concluded what looked at the time like a humiliating peace treaty with the Ottomans in 1590; in reality, however, it allowed him to focus his military energies on a war with the Uzbeks. Abbas's plan paid off and soon he was able to recapture Herat and stabilize the eastern frontier.

Only then did he confront the Ottomans; Tabriz was retaken in 1605, followed by Baghdad in 1623. By 'Abbas's death in 1629, the Safavid empire had regained the territories claimed for it by the founder of the dynasty.

Abbas also rejuvenated the Iranian economy by entering into trade agreements with foreign powers. Before 'Abbas came to the throne, the Portuguese had established bases in Bahrein and on the island of Hormuz in the Persian Gulf, which diverted trade away from the Persian mainland to the Portuguese-controlled sea routes through the Indian Ocean. The establishment of the British East India Company in 1600, and the agreement reached by the British with the Safavids in 1616 to trade English cloth for Persian silk, helped to break the Portuguese monopoly and reopen overland routes through Persia to international trade. The Safavids were thus drawn into European affairs, either as a conduit for goods from India or as an ally against the Ottoman empire.

On the domestic front, 'Abbas's policies were no less astute. Determined to curb the influence of the Qizilbash once and for all, he established a personal army – the 'slaves of the royal household' – made up of Georgian, Circassian and Armenian prisoners of war who converted to Islam and become Persianized. Loyal only to the shah, the new army supplanted the Qizilbash forces in the field and put down Qizilbash revolts whenever they occurred. Qizilbash chiefs were removed from the major offices of government and their lands seized from the crown, adding revenue with which to finance the reforms. These measures led to a centralization of power in the hands of the shah, and probably thus ensured the survival of the dynasty after his death.

Shah Abbas's achievements were not limited to political and military affairs. A patron of the arts, he presided over a brilliant court, which was moved in 1598 to the new capital, Isfahan, where his patronage helped to nurture an efflorescence of Persian artistic genius. Most brilliant of all was Isfahan itself, which Abbas made his own, adorning the old Seljuk capital with the finest examples of Safavid architecture. Measuring 38 kilometres in circumference and housing over a million people, Isfahan under Shah Abbas became one of the world's greatest and most beautiful cities, home to architectural wonders such as the 'Ali Qapu, or Royal Palace; the Masjid-i Shah, or Royal Mosque; the Mosque of Shaykh Lutfullah; the impressive 4 kilometre long Chahar Bagh avenue, lined by lush gardens and court residences; and the fabulous Maidan, or Central Square, measuring 507 metres long and 158 metres wide, around which the social life of the city revolved. In the words of a European traveller, passing through Iran almost a century after 'Abbas's death, 'When this great prince ceased to live, Persia ceased to prosper'.

THE MOGHULS

It is in India that Islam's third great medieval empire is to be found: the sultanate of the Moghuls.

Islam first made its presence felt in India in the eighth century, when the Muslims conquered Sind. Unable to progress further than the Indus delta, they chose to settle peacefully, causing no great disturbance to the Indian people. Three centuries passed before a Muslim force attacked the subcontinent again. Yet although Mahmud of Ghazna was able to annex the Punjab, Multan and part of Sind early in the eleventh century, Indian life – and, more importantly, Indian religion – continued more or less as it had before. All of this changed with the arrival at the end of the twelfth century of a tribe of Turkish warriors, the Khaljis. This was unlike all other Muslim invasions in that its architects intended not just to raid and retreat, but to stay and rule. Within a few decades, they had established a sultanate in Delhi, from where they ruled the whole of the Ganges valley. They were unable to take Islam much further south, however, and Hindu society survived there largely unhindered.

The stability of the Muslim rulers in the north of India did not last long, however, and following the devastation wrought by Timur in 1398, Muslim India fragmented again; and while new Muslim rulers did occasionally emerge at Delhi, they lacked the power to revive the former Islamic sultanate. The reversal of Muslim fortunes in India did not happen until the sixteenth century, when the old empire was restored by an outsider, Babur of Kabul.

Babur was a Chagatai prince, descended on his father's side from Timur and on his mother's side from Genghis Khan. Unable to establish himself as ruler of his native Samarkand, Babur turned his attention to Afghanistan and from there to India. From his base in Kabul he gained control of the Punjab, and in 1526 defeated the Delhi *sultan* Ibrahim Lodi at the battle of Panipat. The following year he defeated the Hindu Rajput confederacy, and in 1529 routed the Afghans of eastern Uttar Pradesh and Bihar. By the time of his death in 1530, most of northern India was under his control. In this way the foundations of the Moghul empire were laid.[10]

The Moghul dynasty, which would rule over most of India for two and a half centuries, was noted for the ability of its rulers and the efficacy of its administration. Furthermore, the first Moghul emperors were men of high culture and sophistication, with interests in architecture, music and literature which distinguished them from previous Muslim rulers of India. More important, though, was the Moghul policy of toleration towards non-Muslims – initiated by Babur and continued by most of his successors – and the attempt to integrate Hindus and Muslims into a united state. Religious tolerance was to become a hallmark of the Moghul empire in its heyday.

Babur's son Humayun (r. 1530–42 and 1554–6) lost control of the empire temporarily to Sher Khan, the Afghan, in 1542, but eventually recaptured the Delhi throne twelve years later. When he died in 1556, allegedly after a fall on the library stairs, he was succeeded by the greatest of all the Moghuls, Akbar the Great.

Akbar's fifty-year reign (1556–1605) marked the zenith of Moghul power in India. An able warrior, he succeeded in annexing all of northern India and much of the central heartland, while maintaining Babur's policy of toleration towards the Hindu subjects of the realm, to the point of employing them in his army and government apparatus. For his time, Akbar was also a radical free-thinker, with ideas that did not endear him to the conservative *ulama* of the day. One such idea was for a new religious creed – the so-called *din-i ilahi*, or 'divine religion' – which was a mish-mash of Zoroastrianism, Islam and Hinduism. It did not catch on. A capable administrator, Akbar set up enlightened political and administrative structures that ensured the survival of the dynasty for at least another century and a half. By the time of his death in 1605, the Moghul empire stretched from Afghanistan in the west to the Bay of Bengal in the east, and southward to Gujarat and the Deccan.

Akbar's son, Jahangir (r. 1605–27), built upon his father's foundations, developing further the already successful administrative system and continuing the tolerant policy towards Hindus. The first part of his reign was thus a successful one, with a steady growth of trade and commerce and a great flowering of the arts. The second part of his reign, however, was characterized by a series of rebellions against his rule, orchestrated primarily by his sons, and it was thanks to the support of his wife, the empress Nur Jahan, that he was able to survive. He was succeeded by his son, Shah Jahan (r. 1628–58), the last of the great Moghul emperors. A ruthless but competent ruler, Shah Jahan presided over a court that was unmatched in its brilliance. His most famous legacy is, of course, the Taj Mahal, built as a tomb for his beloved third wife, Mumtaz Mahal, and hailed today as possibly the most magnificent monument in the Muslim world. Shah Jahan's reign marked the cultural pinnacle of Moghul rule, but his military campaigns – two wars in the Deccan, the subjugation of Bijapur and numerous attacks on the Uzbeks and the Persians – brought the empire to the verge of bankruptcy.

FOUR

The Modern Era

THE DECLINE OF THE THREE EMPIRES

The three great empires – the Ottoman, the Safavid and the Moghul – peaked at approximately the same time; now, in the mid-seventeenth century, they were all on the decline together.

In Safavid Iran, signs that all was not well first began to show after the death of Shah Abbas I; indeed, some historians have pointed an accusing finger at Abbas himself, blaming the problems that were later to beset the dynasty on the very measures he had taken to make his own reign such a success. The personal 'slave army' that he had created as a means of curbing the power of the tribes proved to be less than competent on the battlefield; more importantly, the requisition of state lands by the crown to finance this army led to crippling over-taxation and the concomitant weakening of provincial administration.

It was with the death of Shah 'Abbas I in 1629 that the rot really began to set in. The four rulers who succeeded him were, without exception, men whose focus was more on the pleasures of the chase or the tavern than the exigencies of statecraft. It did not help, of course, that since Shah 'Abbas's reign it had been customary to cloister the princes of the realm in the harem. While this achieved the desired effect of preventing the shah's offspring from being used by unscrupulous courtiers to plot against him, it did mean that when they finally emerged as rulers in their own right, they did so with little experience of the outside world and virtually no awareness of the demands of kingship. Corrupted by the hedonism of harem life, the four shahs who succeed 'Abbas I to the Safavid throne – namely Shah Safi (1629–42), 'Abbas II (1642–66), Sulayman (1666–94) and Shah Sultan Husayn (1694–1722) – have been portrayed as perpetual drunkards, manipulated by self-seeking courtiers and ambitious Shi'ite clerics. Of these four, only 'Abbas II showed any of his earlier namesake's aplomb as a ruler.

The degeneration of Safavid kingship went hand-in-glove with the rise to predominance in Safavid society of the Shi'ite *ulama*. Their financial and ideological independence of the crown increased throughout the period, as did the inability – and, at times, unwillingness – of the monarchy to do anything about it. Furthermore, after the first hundred years of Safavid rule, the religious legitimacy which the dynasty had enjoyed since its inception began to be called into question. The three basic stances vis-à-vis the government hitherto discernible among the Shi'ite *ulama* – quietistic rejection, cautious accommodation and unquestioning endorsement – were joined at the end of the seventeenth century by a fourth: unequivocal ideological opposition to monarchical rule. According to at least one Shi'ite scholar of the time, the Safavid shahs had no 'divine right' to rule, whether they were descended from the House of Ali or not; in the absence of the Hidden Imam,[11] authority belonged to the most learned jurist of the age, and to no one else.

Without a fully developed ethos of government on which to base their claims, the few dissenting voices largely went unheard; the concept of 'government by jurist' would have to wait another three centuries before emerging as a credible alternative to monarchical rule. Nevertheless, the fact that such an idea was voiced when it was demonstrates the growing confidence and autonomy of thought of some of the Shi'ite *ulama* in the Safavid period. And although no Shi'ite theocracy rose up to supplant the Safavid usurpers, the strength of their social base and the virtual stranglehold they enjoyed on the later Safavid rulers meant that, for all intents and purposes, they were the real power behind the throne, if not rulers in their own right. At no time was this more evident than during the reign of Shah Sultan Husayn (r. 1694–1722). Torn between the pleasure of the harem and the piety of the prayer-niche, the weak and ineffectual Husayn presided over a court whose power lay almost unquestionably in the hands of the *ulama*, in particular the notorious Muhammad Baqir Majlisi (1037–1110). In an attempt to impose his own vision of Shi'ite orthodoxy on the population, Majlisi set out to cleanse Safavid society of all traces of what he and his supporters considered to be 'heterodox'. Consequently, Sufism was denounced as a 'hellish growth' and Sufi adherents were persecuted. Philosophy and theosophy were deemed unfit for intellectual consumption by Muslims, and similarly those involved in such 'heretical' disciplines were also hounded. While his supporters have portrayed Majlisi as a reformer, others have denounced him as a narrow-minded obscurantist, responsible for unleashing something akin to a religious inquisition lasting several decades.

However, Majlisi's most vehement attacks were reserved
for his Sunni coreligionists. Indeed, it was the denunciation
of Sunnism and the persecution of the Sunni minority
which, according to some historians, facilitated the conquest
of Isfahan at the hands of the Sunni Afghans in 1722.
Whether Majlisi is partly to blame for the Safavid downfall is
left as a point of historical debate; the fact remains that by
the end of the second decade of the eighteenth century the
dynasty was rotten to the core, and the capture of Isfahan by
the Afghan warrior, Mahmud of Qandahar, was a relatively
straightforward affair. Having failed to create a dynasty of his
own, however, Mahmud later abdicated in favour of a former
rebel from the Afsharid tribe, the Sunni Nadir Khan.
Isfahan, the glorious capital created by Shah Abbas, lay in
ruins as two hundred years of Shi'ite rule came to an
ignominious end.

Crowned in 1736, Nadir Shah promised to restore Iran to its
former greatness. In 1739 he marched into India and captured
Delhi; among the treasures taken as booty was the famous
Peacock Throne, later to grace the palaces of future Iranian
emperors. A northern campaign brought the Transoxanian
khanates of Khiva and Bokhara under Nadir's sway, while in
the south his troops succeeded in capturing most of Oman. Yet
this brief resurgence of Iranian greatness was to come to an
end with Nadir's death in 1748, at which point Iran was
divided among its tribes. Years of anarchy ensued, bringing
lawlessness, bloodshed and poverty in its wake. Tellingly, by the
end of the eighteenth century, only a quarter of Isfahan – the
city once touted as *nesf-e jahan*, or 'half the world' – was
populated. It was not until 1794 that a semblance of order was

restored, this time under the Shi'ite Qajar tribe, but by then the old empire was a shadow of its former self.

While the Safavids were on the wane in Iran, the Moghuls were losing their grip on the Indian subcontinent. Yet unlike its Safavid counterpart, the Moghul empire could not blame its eventual decline on the inherent weakness or degeneracy of its rulers. The emperor Awrangzeb (r. 1658–1707), under whom the rot set in, was renowned as a genuinely pious Muslim and fearless warrior, unsullied by the corruptive influences of the harem. He was also a ruthless pragmatist whose path to the throne was stained by the blood of his father, Shah Jahan, whom he imprisoned, and his three brothers, whom he put to death. The undoing of the Moghuls lay not in any deficiency of will on Awranzgeb's part, but rather on a disastrous policy decision made at the height of his power.

Under previous Moghul rulers, the principle of religious tolerance had been deemed crucial to the smooth running of what was a Muslim empire in an overwhelmingly Hindu society; under Awrangzeb, it was abandoned almost entirely. Heavily influenced by the *ulama* of the day, who had begun to question the religious compromises on which the empire rested, Awrangzeb reimposed the *jizya* on non-Muslims and attempted to outlaw the Hindu religion and destroy its temples. Antagonism towards these measures manifested itself in a series of popular revolts by those groups – Hindus, Sikhs, Rajputs in particular – for whom Awrangzeb's Islamicizing zeal spelt disaster.

By far the most serious challenge to Moghul authority came from the Marathas, a Scytho-Dravidian peoples who, under their charismatic leader, Shivaji (1627–80), had set up a Hindu state in the Deccan and refused to be coopted into the empire or to exist peacefully alongside it. In 1680 Awrangzeb embarked on a series of campaigns into the Deccan in order to quell the Marathan threat, but by the time he died in 1707, very little headway had been made, and the Marathas were still able to carry out successful raiding expeditions from Gujarat to the southern tip of the subcontinent.

After Awrangzeb's death, the ruling class began to disintegrate and within several decades the Moghul empire had ceased to exist as an effective political unit. Various factions, each supporting a rival claimant to the throne, vied with each other for supremacy. As centralized authority declined, there came into existence a whole host of new kingdoms and principalities, created by Hindu and Muslim opportunists, and a number of large independent states such as Hyderabad and Bengal, headed by former governors of the imperial provinces. In 1739 the ailing Moghul regime suffered further humiliation when Nadir Shah invaded India and plundered Delhi. Although the Persian ruler later withdrew, in 1761 Delhi was sacked again, this time by the invading forces of Ahmad, king of Afghanistan (r. 1747–73).

When the Afghans left in 1764, the Moghul emperor Shah Alam (1759–1806) regained his throne, but he was to be ruler in name alone. All around him, non-Muslims were taking control of India. By 1800 the Marathas ruled from the deserts of Rajasthan in the north to the Deccan in the south; from the Arabian sea in the west to the Bay of Bengal in the east. The Sikh leader, Ranjit Singh (1780–1839) – the 'Lion of the Punjab' – became ruler of Lahore in 1801 before going on to become the most powerful ruler in India. In 1764, the British

East India Company became formal ruler of Bengal, the first in a long series of acquisitions upon which the British Raj was built. By the turn of the nineteenth century, Muslim rule was restricted to Awadh and Hyderabad, and even these states recognized the paramountcy of the British. The decline of Muslim authority in India was recognized by one of the leading Delhi *ulama*, who announced in 1803 that India was no longer *dar al-Islam*, 'the abode of Islam', but *dar al-harb*, 'the abode of war'. The thousand-year rule of Muslims in India was over.

A stronger entity than either of its Safavid or Moghul contemporaries, the Ottoman empire took much longer to expire, its gradual decline spanning some three hundred years. The concept of decline is, of course, difficult to pin down, and in the case of the Ottoman empire should be seen primarily in relation to its own 'golden age' under Sulayman, and to the remarkable progress being made at the time by its European neighbours.

From the sixteenth century onwards certain developments in the West highlighted the gulf that was developing between the Ottoman empire and her European neighbours. The growth of overseas trade had enriched western Europe, bringing into existence a prosperous middle class which failed to emerge in the Ottoman empire as a source of support for the ruler; the wealthy bourgeoisie which did exist at the time was small, comprising either non-Muslims, who were unacceptable as allies for the *sultan*, or bureaucrats, who were anxious to serve their own interests and were largely resistant to change. The Ottomans also lagged behind in the fields of science and technology, with innovations that were commonplace in sixteenth-century Europe not reaching Ottoman shores until two centuries later.

The empire's own domestic problems were even more acute. From the death of Sulayman in 1566 to the end of the eighteenth century, the Ottomans were saddled with rulers who, with few exceptions, were unfit to lead an empire. Some were simply incompetent; others, mentally defective. It is not surprising to learn, therefore, that their average rule of thirteen years was less than half that of the first ten Ottoman *sultans*. Like their Safavid counterparts, the Ottoman princes grew up in the harem, cushioned from the realities of the outside world. Many of them were under the influence of the *valide sultan* – the queen mother – and thus the focus of palace intrigue and in-fighting; in fact, for most of the first half of the seventeenth century, the females of the harem were so influential that this period has come to be known as 'The Sultanate of the Women'.

The administration suffered from corruption and nepotism. Whereas promotion in the early years of the empire had been on merit, the purchase of office now became commonplace. Like a cancer, the corruption spread insidiously from Istanbul, the administrative heart of the empire, to the provinces. There, officials would buy their offices, then impose crippling taxes on the local populace to reimburse themselves. Sometimes justice, too, was available only at a price.

Parallel to this was the slow decline of the Ottoman military machine. The *devshirme* was abandoned and the Janissaries were weakened in the process. More importantly, the provincial cavalry was being made obsolescent by the musket-armed troops of Europe. This meant that the Ottomans would have to increase their standing infantry and equip them with firearms. All of this required money. However, the ailing economy made further military reforms an impossibility. Inflation raged as New World silver flowed in, fuelling further corruption and economic havoc. As the Europeans tightened their control of new sea trade routes to India, bypassing the old land routes of the Middle East, the Ottoman trade balance worsened. Although the empire would not earn the epithet 'Sick Man of Europe' for another hundred years or more, in the two centuries following Sulayman's demise it was certainly beginning to show symptoms of chronic malaise.

However, a dynasty that had seen three hundred years of continuous growth and prosperity was not going to surrender to terminal illness without a fight, and in the latter part of the seventeenth century there were concerted efforts made by the more enlightened at court to halt the decline. At the forefront of these endeavours was the illustrious Koprolu family of viziers, who strove valiantly to weed out corruption and bring back a semblance of efficiency to the administration and the military. So successful were they, in fact, that in 1663 the Ottomans were able to besiege Vienna for the second time. Yet the resurgence, such as it was, proved to be short-lived. On the horizon a host of opponents – Austria, Poland, Russia, Iran – stood ready to challenge the Ottoman regime, often in alliance. In 1699 defeat by a coalition of European powers obliged the Ottomans to sign the Treaty of Karlowitz, in which they surrendered territories in the Balkans. This was the first time that they had entered into a peace treaty as the defeated power, and it would not be the last. The Treaty of Passarowitz, signed in 1718, saw further losses, including Serbia. In 1768 Russia inflicted a series of damaging defeats on the Ottomans, both on land and at sea, culminating in the humiliating Treaty of Kuchuk Kainarji in 1774. According to the terms of the treaty, not only did the Ottomans lose control of a large swathe of Black Sea shore, they were also forced to relinquish political control for the first time over a wholly Muslim people, the Crimean Tatars. The shrinking of the Ottoman empire had begun.

The gradual political decline of the Muslims in the seventeenth and eighteenth centuries provided the backdrop for one of the most important developments in Islam for several centuries. This was the growth of a revivalist movement, fuelled by a spirit of religious renewal and regeneration, which began in the middle of the eighteenth century and spread to virtually every part of the Muslim world. The movement had as many variations as there were different Islamic communities and traditions: in some areas it was spearheaded by the orthodox *ulama*, in others by the mainstream Sufi brotherhoods. Yet however it manifested itself, the movement had but one message: the cause of the decline of the Muslim world is the decline of Islam itself. The true practice of Islam, it was argued, had been sullied by centuries of foreign, unislamic accretions and innovations, while the continued closure of the 'gate of *ijtihad*' had led to the ossification of Islamic law, thus robbing Islam of its dynamism. As a result, Muslims had fallen away from the true path. To halt this decline, Muslims must therefore return to the first principles – the Koran and the *sunna* – for guidance, thus reviving the pure faith of the Prophet and his companions.

The first major manifestation of the Islamic revival in the eighteenth century was the Wahhabi movement, named after its founder, Muhammad ibn 'Abd al-Wahhab (1703–92). Trained in Hanbali law and the teachings of the ultraorthodox jurist and theologian, Ibn Taymiyya (d. 1328), 'Abd al-Wahhab considered the social conditions of his time to be little better than those of the 'age of ignorance' – the *jahiliyya* – which preceded Islam. Appalled by the superstitions, innovations and suspect practices of the general population, such as the worship of saints and the veneration of shrines, he called for a complete revival of Islam along the lines of the pristine faith practised by Muhammad in Medina. He also advocated armed revolt against the Ottomans. In 1744 he joined forces with a local tribal leader, Muhammad b. Saud (d. 1765), and created a militant revivalist movement that swept like a fire through the Arabian peninsula. In Mecca and Medina, the tombs of the Prophet and his companions were levelled; in the Shi'ite holy city of Karbala, the shrine of Imam Husayn was destroyed and many Shi'ite pilgrims were massacred. By the beginning of the nineteenth century, the Wahhabi movement was in control of most of Arabia, and its influence widely felt throughout most of the Muslim world.

In the Indian subcontinent, Shah Wali Allah of Delhi (1703–62) played a similar role to that of 'Abd al-Wahhab, albeit with some important differences. Shah Wali Allah espoused a form of Sufism – he was an adherent of the Naqshbandiyya brotherhood – from which foreign accretions and popular superstitions had been removed. This 'purified' Sufism would do in Moghul India, and much of the rest of the Muslim world, what 'Abd al-Wahhab's fundamentalist orthodoxy did in Arabia: it would posit a return to the pristine Islam of the Prophet as the only way of solving the problems of the day. Like 'Abd al-Wahhab, Shah Wali Allah advocated a return to *ijtihad* as outlined by Ibn Taymiyya.

Elsewhere in the Muslim world, the spirit of revivalism grew apace. In Africa a series of revivalist movements culminated in the formation of several Islamic states, such as those of Uthman Dan Fodio in Nigeria (1754–1817), the Sanusiyya in Libya (1787–1859), and the Sudanese Mahdi (1848–85). In central and south-eastern Asia, too, similar trends were observable, with a whole rash of revivalist movements springing up throughout the eighteenth and nineteenth centuries.

Ultimately, however, the challenge was too great. For not only did Muslims have to grapple with their own internal demons, they also had to face up to an even greater threat from outside: the spectre of European colonialism. It is to the advance of Europe that we now turn.

THE NINETEENTH CENTURY: EUROPEAN COLONIALISM AND THE MUSLIM RESPONSE

The decline of the three great Islamic empires in the eighteenth century was paralleled by the acceleration of technical and economic development in the West, culminating in the Industrial Revolution and the ascendancy of the European nations in the fields of commerce, trade, industry and technology. The Muslim world lagged behind in all of these areas, and could only watch with envy and consternation as Europe, for so long overshadowed by the brilliance of Islamic civilization, now began to outpace it on every front. More importantly, the West's maritime might and military prowess were such that at the close of the eighteenth century it was ready not only to outstrip the Muslim world economically but also to dominate it politically. As the nineteenth century dawned, so did the era of European colonialism; by the end of the nineteenth century, much of the Muslim Middle East – and the Islamic world beyond – was either directly under the control of the West or in various ways affected irreversibly by Western or Westernizing influences.

The final stages in the demise of the Ottoman empire began with Napoleon Bonaparte's occupation of Egypt (1798–1801) – the first time since the Crusades that a European power had taken possession of part of the Muslim world. Although the French did not stay in Egypt for long, they were to have a lasting impact on the elite strata of Egyptian society. The power vacuum left by the departure of Napoleon's forces was filled by the Albanian military officer, Muhammad Ali (1769–1849), whom the Ottomans acknowledged as viceroy of Egypt (1805–48). Muhammad Ali embarked on a French-inspired programme of modernisation that had virtually no precedent in the Muslim world. He confiscated religious endowments (*awqaf*), formed a regular army on European lines, and dispatched a number of educational missions to various parts of Europe. When the Wahhabis invaded Iraq and went on to capture Mecca and Medina, the Ottoman Sultan Mahmud II (r. 1808–39) called on Muhammad Ali to crush the rebellion. His victory over the Wahhabis strengthened his position and enabled him to rule Egypt almost independently. It also made him more ambitious; so ambitious, in fact, that he later rebelled against his Ottoman overlords and annexed Syria. It is possible that he would have overthrown the *sultan* himself, had the European powers at Mahmud's behest not stepped in to repulse him. Syria was handed back to the Ottomans in 1840, while the Europeans were rewarded for their intervention with enough mercantile concessions to give them virtual control over the whole of the Ottoman empire. From the mid-nineteenth century onwards, the disintegration of the empire gained worrying momentum. Greece gained its independence in 1830, with Serbia following suit a year later. Between 1830 and 1847, Algeria was wrested out of Ottoman hands by the French. Bulgaria became an independent entity in 1878, the same year that Austria seized Bosnia and Herzegovina. Tunisia was made a French protectorate in 1881, while its neighbour Libya was conquered by Italy on the eve of the First World War, by which time most of Ottoman empire's remaining European territories were lost in the Balkan conflicts of 1912–13.

In an effort to remedy the malaise which would, if not checked, cause the Ottoman empire to fall entirely into the hands of European powers, Sultan Abdul Majid (r.1839–61) embarked on a series of westernizing reforms known as the Tanzimat (lit. 'reorganization'). Under the terms of the 'Noble Rescript' (*Hatt-i Sherif*), issued in 1839, all religious groups were henceforth to be regarded as equal before the law. This marked a radical break with Ottoman Islamic tradition, which had always regarded non-Muslims as separate and inferior. In 1856 equal treatment of Muslims and non-Muslims was guaranteed once more by the 'Imperial Rescript' (*Hatt-i Homayun*); in 1867 Christians, who made up 40 per cent of the *sultan's* subjects, began to be appointed to state councils. This obvious move towards complete integration was followed by radical changes in the legal and educational systems, hitherto both controlled by the ulama. From 1840 oneards, Western-style counrts and legal codes were introduced and the administration was restructured along French lines. The educational system was also overhauled, with new secular institutions of learnine designed to produce elites who would, in turn, carry on the process of reform.

Attention was also paid to the country's infrastructure: land was reclaimed and new factories and workshops were built; postal and telegraph systems were set up; and a railway was established. The Tanzimat reforms were the most far-reaching yet attempted in the Muslim world, and easily the most revolutionary. Yet if the purpose behind them was to build the empire up to a point where it might compete on its own terms with its European adversaries, then it may be argued that they were an abject failure. For all the reforms appeared to secure was the triumph of Europe over the Ottoman empire thanks to the imposition, often with the aid of European advisers and experts, of European institutions and practices.

Abdul Majid was succeeded by his brother, Abdul Aziz (r.1861–76), who continued the westernizing reforms and, in doing so, drove the Ottoman empire to the brink of bankruptcy. The loans he used to finance his schemes were taken from Western banks, thus giving European governments and their financiers a hitherto unprecedented degree of control over the empire's economy. Under Abdulhamid II (1876–1909), Ottoman fortunes went from bad to worse. While the Tanzimat reforms had culminated in the Constitution of 1876, the damaging 1877–8 war with Russia and the Treaty of Berlin, as a result of which most of the empire's European lands were lost and European powers laid claim to various spheres of influence in the Middle East, presented Abdulhamid with the pretext he needed to bring an end to liberalization and proceed with reforms as he saw fit, namely under his own autocratic guidance. By the 1880s, Germany under Kaiser Wilhelm had replaced France and Great Britain as ally and military advisor of the Ottoman empire, while Abdulhamid himself was drawn to new ideologies such as Pan-Islamism. Abdulhamid's main opponents at home, known collectively as the Young Turks, gravitated to a more secular form of Ottoman nationalism, and it was a revolution staged by the Young Turks in 1908–9 that finally brought an end to Abdulhamid's despotism. Under the Young Turk Committee of Union and Progress, constitutional, parliamentary government was established, reflecting the growing trend towards Turkish nationalism. The Balkan Wars which preceded the First World War brought the military element of the Young Turk movement to the fore, culminating in the domination of the political sphere in Istanbul by the so-called 'Young Turk Triumvirate' of Enver, Talat and Jemal Pasha, who led the Ottomans into the First World War on the side of the Germans. The Turkish defeat in the war finally discredited the Young Turks, however, and paved the way for the rise of a new nationalist movement under the leadership of an army officer named Mustafa Kemal, later to be known as Ataturk or 'Father of the Turks'. Under Ataturk, the nationalist government began to take Turkey in the direction of secularism and Westernization; to this end, Turkey became an independent republic in 1923, abolishing the caliphate a year later. The 600-year reign of the Ottomans was finally over.

Abdul Aziz's mismanagement of the Ottoman economy was paralleled by that of the Khedive Ismail, who ruled Egypt from 1863 to 1879. Ismail's modernizing zeal outstripped even that of his grandfather, Muhammad Ali, and was to find ample expression in his construction of the Suez Canal in 1869. The crippling expenditure on this and other projects, such as railways and an opera house, led to the accumulation of a heavy foreign debt: with bankruptcy looming, Egypt was forced to surrender to Franco-British financial control. A nationalist uprising – the 'Urabi revolt of 1881–2 – provoked British intervention; two years later, Britain appointed a Consul-General, Earl Cromer, who was effectively the ruler of Egypt until 1907. British involvement in the area did not end with Egypt, however, for Britain also showed an interest in the Ottoman empire's other Arab subjects, especially those who were disillusioned with Ottoman rule and bent on achieving autonomy; one such example was the Sharif of Mecca. Britain made it clear that as far as the issue of independence was concerned, she was on the side of the Arabs and ready to help them in every way possible. What she did not reveal, however, was the fact that any support she might give the Arabs in their quest for freedom stemmed not from altruism but from political self-interest: in 1916, unbeknownst to the Arabs, Britain had signed the infamous Sykes-Picot agreement, which was basically a blueprint for the carving up of the post-Ottoman Middle East into British and French spheres of influence. At the end of the First World War, the Sharif of Mecca became King Husayn of the Hejaz, while five new, largely artificial political entities – Jordan, Iraq, Palestine, Lebanon and Syria – were created out of other parts of the former Ottoman empire. Husayn's two sons became kings of Jordan and Iraq, albeit under British protection. Palestine was governed directly by British mandate, while Syria and Lebanon were ruled by the French.

The situation to the east of the Ottoman empire was somewhat different. While Iran was not formally colonised by any European power at this time, she was the subject of intense Anglo-Russian rivalry throughout the nineteenth century. Weak central government made it relatively easily for Russia to take control of Caucasia and Azerbaijan, while Nasiruddin Shah (1848–96) and his infatuation with all things Western opened the way for Britain to gain a foothold in the south by dint of various commercial monopolies granted by the Persian throne. The commercial stranglehold on Iran enjoyed by both Russia and Britain was completed in 1872, when Baron de Reuters was given vast concessions on banking and mining. Opposition to Western influence and interference in Iran was spearheaded mainly by the Shi'ite *ulama*. When, in 1890, a British consortium was granted a monopoly on the production and sale of tobacco, the leading Shi'ite cleric of the day issued a famous *fatwa*, declaring the use of tobacco to be religiously unlawful. The edict was universally obeyed both in Iran and other areas with Shi'ite populations, and as a result the concession was overturned. The involvement of the Shi'ite clergy in politics continued into the next century, with the *ulama* playing an important role in the constitutional revolution of 1905. Thereafter, however, Iran became increasingly secular and Western-oriented, with the British-appointed Reza Khan ascending the throne in 1925. As Reza Shah, the new ruler curbed the power of the *ulama*, banned the wearing of Islamic dress for both men and women, and embarked on a series of Western-inspired social, educational and political reforms.

Beyond the frontiers of the Ottoman empire and Iran, the rest of the Muslim world was subjected to the depredations of Europe to varying degrees throughout the nineteenth century. In Central Asia, the second half of the century saw Russia extend her territories considerably, swallowing up the ancient khanates of Khiva and Bukhara, the khanate of Khokhand, and the territories known today as Kazakhstan, Tajikistan and Turkmenistan. Further south, Britain had achieved control in India by 1820, giving both Muslims and Hindus the freedom to follow their faiths in accordance with the policy of 'divide and rule'. Towards the end of the century, Britain also achieved hegemony over the Malay states, just as the Dutch were completing their colonisation of Indonesia. In Africa, the British established an Anglo-Egyptian condominium over the Sudan; and gained control of most of the Sultanate of Sokoto, which was absorbed into the British protectorate of Northern Nigeria. Meanwhile, the colonial endeavours of the French saw much of west Africa come under their control between 1890 and 1912, the year in which Morocco also became a French protectorate.

Just as the internal decline of the three great Muslim empires had provoked strong reactions among Muslim scholars and thinkers during the eighteenth century, leading to revivalist movements such as Wahhabism, European domination of the Muslim world in the nineteenth century struck a similar chord, with differing results. Protest sometimes took the form of uprisings – bracketed under the category of *jihad,* or defensive 'holy war' – against the Europeans: notable examples include the *jihad* of the south-east Asians against the Dutch; that of the Sanussi Brotherhood against Italian rule in Libya; and the Mahdist movement in the Sudan. In other parts of the Muslim world, the *ulama* took part in constitutional revolutions, such as that which occurred in Iran between 1905–11. Underpinning most of these movements was a strong pan-Islamic sentiment that drew on early conceptions of the Muslim umma as the basic focus of Islamic solidarity. The most prominent pan-Islamist was the politician, political agitator and journalist Jamal al-Din al-Afghani (1839–97). A mysterious figure about whose life and activities a definitive portrait has yet to emerge, the Iranian-born al-Afghani travelled the length and breadth of the Muslim world, warning against the blind pursuit of Westernization and arguing that the blame for the weakness of Muslims stemmed not from Islam but from Muslims themselves. The vast majority of Muslims, he asserted, had lost touch with the spirit of moral, intellectual and scientific excellence that had made possible the great Islamic empires of the past. Furthermore, he argued that the greatness of Islam could be recaptured with the help of Western technology and learning, but only if Muslims retained their own spiritual and cultural moorings. Without a reconstructed vision of Islam, he argued, Muslims would never be able to regain the vitality they had possessed when they were a dominant force on the world stage, united in a single international community and unaffected by differences of language, culture or outlook. Al-Afghani influenced Muslim thought in Central Asia, Ottoman Turkey and India, and his teachings influenced not only the 1881 revolt in Egypt but also the whole constitutional movement in Iran.

Muhammad 'Abduh (1849–1905), al-Afghani's disciple, argued along the same lines. Rector of the famous al-Azhar university, 'Abduh argued that the Muslim world had been subjugated to the forces of the West not because of any weakness on the part of Islam, but because most Muslims were bad Muslims. The main cause of Muslim backwardness, claimed 'Abduh, was the scourge of *taqlid*, or blind acceptance, be it of legal precepts or fundamentals of faith. What was needed, 'Abduh asserted, was a return to the true Islam of the Koran and the *sunna*, to the pure beliefs and practices of 'the righteous forefathers' (*al-salaf al-salih*). The reform movement inspired by his teachings came to be known as the Salafiyya, and was influential throughout the Muslim world. Identifying with an ideal time in history – the 'Golden Age' of the Prophet and the Righteous Caliphs, the Salafiyya advocated past-oriented change to bring present-day Muslims up to the standards of the earlier ideal, albeit in a way that was reconcilable with the spirit of social and scientific progressiveness demonstrated by the West.

DECOLONIZATION AND NEO-REVIVALISM

If the nineteenth century was one long litany of woes for Muslims, with most parts of their world coming under direct European domination, the advent of the twentieth century brought new hope. Signs that Muslim fortunes were improving came after the First World War. The Ottoman Turks and the Iranians, never formally colonized by the European powers, had begun to solve their internal problems and slowly master their affairs. It now remained for the vast majority of the Muslim peoples who had not been able to escape European domination to take their destinies into their own hands. The process of decolonization which took place throughout the Islamic world in the first half of the twentieth century served precisely that purpose, allowing most Muslims the opportunity of liberation from the direct political control of the Europeans.

Egypt was the first of the former Ottoman territories to achieve independence. When Turkey entered the First World War as an ally of Germany, Britain declared Egypt a protectorate, promising a degree of political change once the war was over. Buoyed by the thought of achieving self-determination, Egyptian nationalists formed the Wafd (lit. 'delegation') movement in 1918 to plan for the country's independence. Britain, however, reneged on her promises; the leader of the Wafd, Sa'd Zaghloul, was exiled and the Egyptian people rose up in violent revolt. Unrest continued until 1922, when Britain finally declared Egypt an independent monarchy under King Fuad I.

The modern kingdom of Saudi Arabia came into existence several years later. Emerging from exile in Kuwait, the Saud dynasty recaptured their old capital, Riyadh, in 1902; by 1906 Abdul Aziz ibn Saud's forces enjoyed complete control over the Nejd. He took the Hasa region in 1913, the Jabal Shammar in 1921, Mecca in 1924, Medina in 1925 and Asir in 1926. He then proclaimed himself king of the Hejaz, before going on to reunify the conquered territories and, in 1932, renaming his kingdom Saudi Arabia.

Iraq, Syria, Jordan and Lebanon – largely artificial states that had been created out of former Ottoman territories in the aftermath of the First World War – were next in line. A former British mandate, Iraq joined the League of Nations as a free and independent state in the autumn of 1932. Syria became a charter member of the United Nations in 1945, after uprisings had led to British military intervention and the subsequent removal of all French forces and administrative personnel. A year later, Britain gave up her mandate over Transjordan, which was duly recognized as a sovereign independent state and renamed Jordan four years later. Also in 1946 Lebanon saw the evacuation of the last French troops from its soil, thus heralding that country's full independence.

Elsewhere in the Muslim world, the move towards independence continued apace after the Second World War. Pakistan came into existence in 1947, followed two years later by Indonesia. Libya became an independent monarchy in 1951. In 1956 Morocco and Tunisia emerged from years of French colonial control and gained independence; Sudan attained its freedom from Britain and Egypt the same year. Malaya became an independent state in 1957, while in 1960 a whole host of African nations with considerable Muslim populations – Mali, Mauritania, Niger, Nigeria, Somalia and Upper Volta (now Burkina Faso) – gained autonomy. Finally, in 1962, Algeria was able to throw off the shackles of French rule, albeit only after an eight-year war of independence that had resulted in over a million Algerian casualties, and almost two million refugees.

One development which ran counter to the general process of decolonization, and which was to usher in decades of unrest and strife throughout the Muslim world, was the creation of the state of Israel on Palestinian soil in 1948. The British had wrested Palestine from the Ottoman Turks at the end of the First World War, aided by the Arabs, to whom they promised independence once the war was over. However, Britain made two other promises which ran totally at odds with this: in the Sykes–Picot agreement with France and Russia (1916) she had vowed to carve up the region and rule it along with her allies; in the Balfour Declaration, made a year later, Britain promised the Jews a 'national home' in Palestine. The latter promise was the one that was upheld when Palestine came under British mandate in 1922. Not surprisingly, the Arab Palestinians rejected the British right to sign their land away to a third party, and a series of anti-Zionist uprisings ensued. Britain denounced Zionist claims to the whole of Palestine, but reconfirmed their support for the Jews and their creation of a new national home. Despite Arab revolts and measures taken by the British to limit the number of Jews entering Palestine, Jewish immigration increased, especially after the Second World War. Unable to find a solution to the problem it had created, Britain finally deemed the mandate impracticable and, in April 1947, called on the United Nations to review the matter.

Despite the fact that the number of native Palestinians was double that of the Jews, the latter had the upper hand in the showdown that ensued. Backed by a semi-autonomous government, led by the socialist David Ben-Gurion (1886–1973), and a competent military organization, the

Haganah, the Jews were far better prepared than the Arabs, who had never really recovered from the revolts that had taken place a decade earlier. When, in November 1947, the United Nations proposed the partition of Palestine into Jewish and Arab states, the Arabs rejected the plan while the Jews accepted. In the war that followed, the Arabs suffered an ignominious defeat, and on 14 May 1948 the state of Israel was established. Conflict between Israel and her Arab neighbours has been a constant feature of Middle Eastern history ever since, with the staunch support offered to the Zionist state by western nations – the United States in particular – serving as ample proof to many Muslims of the West's determination to maintain a tangible presence, albeit by proxy, in the very heartlands of the Muslim Middle East.

Although most of the Islamic world had thrown off the colonial yoke of Europe by the mid-twentieth century, for many Muslims the whole process of decolonization appeared to be little more than a shambolic façade: a cosmetic exercise designed to lull the Muslim masses into a false sense of security. While independent Muslim states emerged one after the other with welcome rapidity, the underlying and increasingly unpalatable truth was lost on no one: in the vast majority of cases, the individuals, groups and parties that had shaken off the shackles of European domination and led their lands to freedom were, more often than not, members of the Western-educated – and, *ipso facto*, Western-oriented – elite. Although their rise to power did indeed signal the formal end of European control over the Muslim Middle East, the fact that they were largely products of the West meant that it was relatively easy for Europe – and, increasingly, the USA – to continue to dominate the region by proxy. Economic aid and the promotion of industrial, agricultural and educational projects were but a few of the mechanisms employed by western powers to retain a degree of control over their former colonies. Gradually it became clear to all but those too blinkered to see that they had not got rid of the West at all.

The development of a nominally independent Muslim Middle East was paralleled by the rise of a marked neorevivalist trend, fuelled partly by the growing realization that the Muslim world was, its apparent independence notwithstanding, still subject to implicit western hegemony. The aim of the neorevivalists was nothing less than a complete transformation of society along Islamic lines; to this end, they blended the ethics of the Koran with overt – and at times radical – social activism. For the neorevivalists, Islam is a complete way of life, an all-embracing ideology capable of lifting the Muslim world from its morass of ignorance, factionalism and superstition. However, unlike the modernist reformers a century earlier, they did not reinterpret Islam to accommodate Western ideas. According to Esposito, 'unlike Islamic modernists who looked to the West and provided an Islamic rationale for the appropriation of Western learning, these contemporary revivalists emphasized the perfection and comprehensiveness of Islam'.[12]

Neorevivalism is epitomized by two movements whose influences have lasted until the present day: the Muslim Brotherhood (Ikhwan al-Muslimin) and the Islamic Society (Jama'at-i Islami). The Muslim Brotherhood was founded in 1928 by an Egyptian schoolteacher, Hasan al-Banna (1906–49). Begun initially as a youth group, from the outset its emphasis was on moral regeneration. However, with the growth of Zionist activity in Palestine, it began to espouse more overtly political ideals, and in 1939 it was transformed into a political party. Its aims were simple: to liberate the Muslim world from foreign domination; and to create a truly Islamic government. In 1948 the Brotherhood was outlawed, ostensibly because it had blamed the Egyptian government for the Israeli victory over the Arabs. This provoked one of the Brotherhood members to assassinate the Egyptian prime minister; in retaliation, al-Banna was murdered by government agents, even though he had personally condemned the assassination. A year later the ban on the Brotherhood was lifted, and for several years there was an uneasy truce between the movement and the government which, in 1952, had overthrown King Farouk. The involvement of the Brotherhood in the attempted assassination of Colonel Nasser in 1954 culminated in the execution of four of its members and the incarceration of several thousand others. As government opposition to the movement intensified, popular support for the Brotherhood increased accordingly, with branches appearing all over the Muslim world.

Parallel to the growth of the Muslim Brotherhood in Egypt was that of the Islamic Society in the Indian subcontinent. The Society was founded in 1941 by Maulana Abu'l Ala Maududi (1903–79), initially as a means of voicing his opposition to the Muslim League's demands for Pakistan, which he regarded as un-Islamic and liable to encourage Hindu nationalism. Following the Partition in 1947, Maududi moved to Pakistan, where the Society became a persistent thorn in the side of the government. Maududi advocated nothing less than the full implementation of the *shari'a*. The resultant Islamic state, he asserted, should be ruled by one man so long as that man adhered to state ideology – the ideology of Islam; in this, he would be assisted by those who are able to interpret the *shari'a*, namely the *ulama*. Political parties would become obsolete, with only Muslims taking part in government. Maududi's programme for an Islamic state was ignored for decades, and it was only after the loss of East Pakistan – Bangladesh – in 1971 that many began to think of Islam as a possible way forward for the state. Maududi remains a popular figure among Muslims some twenty years after his death, and his influence on modern Islamic political thinking cannot be over-estimated.

THE MUSLIM WORLD TODAY

Today, as we enter the third Christian millennium, nominal adherence to Islam is a truly global phenomenon. It is possible to travel from the Atlantic in the West along a wide belt of land that stretches across northern Africa and through the Middle East into Central Asia, before heading southwards to the Pacific across the northern regions of the Indian subcontinent, the Malay peninsula and the Indonesian archipelago, without ever leaving the world of Islam. Today, Muslims constitute a majority of the population in over forty nation states and a sizeable minority in many others, including much of western Europe and North America. And some 1,400 years after the death of the Prophet, the Islamic faith continues to expand, arguably with greater rapidity than any other major world religion.

The migration of huge numbers of Muslims to various parts
of Europe – Turkish 'guest workers' to Germany; Algerians and
Tunisians to France; and vast numbers from the Indian subcontinent to the United Kingdom – has, along with events such
as the increase in oil prices in the mid-seventies and the
concomitant rise of the Arab nations as major players on the
global political arena, ensured a high profile in the West for
Islam and the Muslim world. The vocabulary of Islam, too, is
everywhere, from the *ayatullah* and his *fatwa* in the evening
news, to the neighbourhood *imam* and his campaign to
introduce *halal* meat into the local primary school. Islam has
made itself felt in numerous ways throughout the global
village, with Muslims enjoying a visibility on the world stage
unprecedented in their history.

Unfortunately, however, one of the ways in which the world of
Islam has impacted on the West has little to do with the way
Europeans or Americans as private individuals see their Muslim
next-door neighbours, or engage on an everyday level with their
Muslim friends or colleagues in the workplace. It is an
unpalatable fact that over the past twenty-five years, Muslims in
general have become the focus of an irrefragably negative, and
at times downright savage, press. The Western image of Islam as
a harsh, uncompromising religion that demands strict and
unquestioning obedience from its followers, who, if pushed, will
not hesitate to spread their faith with violence and terror, is one
not confined to the rhetoric of twelfth-century Crusaders: fear
of Islam and Muslims, or 'Islamophobia' as it is currently
known, is sadly as visible today as it was then. Just as pictorial
depictions of Muslims as child-eating demons abounded in the
days of Richard the Lionheart, so too some 800 years later do we

come across ostensibly serious works on Islam whose front covers carry photographs of gun-toting mullahs, or balaclava-clad terrorists, often against the backdrop of blown-up embassies or hijacked airliners. While the responsibility for the creation of this negative image lies largely with the sensationalist tabloid press, which is always ready to prey on its readers' fear of the unknown, much damage has been inflicted by those who presumably should know better: one esteemed academic has, famously, made his name by positing the likelihood of a 'clash of civilisations' – namely the West versus Islam – in the wake of the downfall of the Soviet Union and the disappearance of the 'Russian threat'. The Muslim world, it would now seem, is the new ogre to be feared and held at bay as we approach, in the words of yet another academic, the 'end of history'.

Yet the notion of Islam as a religion that is not averse to using violence in order to realize its goals is not wholly a creation of the Western media. Over the past twenty years there has been a proliferation of avowedly militant and militaristic groups and movements throughout the Muslim world that have used violent means to achieve their aims, be it in internal power struggles such as those in Algeria or Afghanistan, or in struggles, against perceived enemies from without, such as the continuing troubles in occupied Palestine. Other groups, while not overtly violent, are deemed such insofar as they are seen to coerce others into adhering to their ideals and beliefs: various so-called 'Islamic fundamentalist' movements, such as those which have come to power in Iran, Sudan and Afghanistan over the past twenty years, number among them. All of these groups have two main features in common. Firstly, like all revivalists before them, they profess the desire to return their societies to the pristine rule of Islam, and in so doing to ameliorate the myriad problems which have come about as a result of over-hurried modernization, the slavish imitation of alien cultures, and the hegemony of the West; secondly, by dint of the high profile they naturally enjoy on the global political arena, they are constantly and consistently portrayed as representatives and purveyors of Islam. What they represent, however, is not Islam but Islamism: Islam made political and transformed into ideology. One must add, in order to prevent accusations of inaccuracy on the grounds that Islam is inherently political anyway, the rider that such groups represent only one facet of the 'Islamist' outlook. For Islamism, or 'Islamic political activism', comes in a variety of guises, and is not a unified, monolithic whole, as its detractors would portray it. Although it invariably involves and encompasses the politics of power, Islamism is characterised by a substantial diversity. While the goals of the various Islamist groups are similar – and are balanced on the fulcrum that is the restoration of Islamic government – the strategies they adopt in order to implement their goals differ widely. Indeed, there are as many kinds of Islamism as there are of Islam itself.

Islamism is, to a large extent, a by-product of the general reassertion of Muslim identity that has taken place over the past fifty years. This reassertion of identity – the so-called 'Islamic resurgence' – has emerged as a collective response to a whole host of factors both internal and external. The problems of rapid modernization; the inability of local rulers to eradicate poverty; rural-to-urban migration; globalization and the contact with the wider world; and the inability to accommodate new developments and cultures have thrown up problems which, given the failure of secular remedies such as socialism and nationalism, have prompted Muslims to look to their identity as followers of Islam in order to find a solution to their ills.

Between the 1950s and the 1990s, certain events on the wider world stage also acted as a catalyst in the reassertion of Muslim identity. The burning of the al-Aqsa mosque in 1969, for example, sparked off a whole new political movement which culminated in the creation of the Organization of the Islamic Conference (OIC), in which foreign ministers from throughout the Muslim world, together with the Islamic Development Bank and various other institutions dealing with economic, educational, cultural and scientific issues, voiced their concerns about the unity of the Muslim *umma*. Following on from this, universities, religious institutions and professional groups throughout the Muslim world began to pay renewed attention to Islam and its role as a viable sociopolitical alternative to the failed ideologies of the past. The 1967 Arab-Israeli war, while constituting a political set-back, was also important ideologically since it marked a shift from Arab nationalism to a search for some kind of stable Muslim identity that could provide a steady basis for unity and cooperation among the Muslim peoples of the world. And Iran's Islamic Revolution of 1979 was a complete watershed. Whatever one thinks of the direction in which Ayatullah Khumayni's revolution has moved since his death a decade ago, one cannot deny that his anti-Shah movement, and the subsequent creation of the first democratically elected Islamic theocracy in history, provided a huge boost to Muslim morale in all parts of the *umma*, giving Muslims the feeling that Islam is able to respond successfully to the problems of the contemporary Islamic world.

Yet while Islamism attracts all the headlines, there are other social and intellectual currents at play within the Islamic world that are equally worthy of attention. In Iran, for example, where the Islamist experiment is taken by outsiders as paradigmatic, the revolutionary zeal of the first decade of the Islamic revolution has, in recent years, given way to a more pragmatic and conciliatory approach to domestic and international issues – a realpolitik anchored in the growing awareness that international neighbours have to be lived with, sociopolitical and economic realities accepted, and ideological adversaries often accommodated if the affairs of Islamic government are to run smoothly.

The gradual rehabilitation of Iran, which has been moving in a more democratic direction for some years now, is partly a result of the natural recognition of limits that all revolutionary movements eventually reach. It is also partly a result of the growth – both inside Iran but also throughout the rest of the Muslim world – of a new reformist trend among Muslim thinkers and academics which draws strength from Islam's innate capacity for self-renewal and the same spirit of critical analysis and self-criticism that fuelled both the revivalist movement at the end of the eighteenth century and the modernist movement at the end of the nineteenth. Known as 'Islamic liberalism' or 'liberal Islam', this largely intellectual movement has grown out of the thoughts and writings of certain Muslim academics who are committed to Islam on the one hand, but who consider Islamism to be misrepresentative of the Koranic ideal. This, they argue, not only connotes a liberal understanding of the Islamic revelation, but also actively commands man to follow liberal positions in all matters Islamic. Thus it is that supporters of 'liberal Islam' champion issues such as the freedom of speech, the freedom to choose one's religion and not be coerced into following Islamic law if one is not a true believer, and the freedom to practise *ijtihad* – all of which, they claim, are upheld by the Koran itself. Other concerns they discuss include the question of democracy, the separation of 'church' and state, the real meaning and role of secularism, the issue of gender and the rights of women, the position of religious minorities, and environmentalism and the notion of human progress.

Liberal Islam is a thriving concern, aided by rising education throughout the Islamic world, by the growing trend of democratisation, and by the disenchantment that many educated Muslims feel with the direction taken by political Islam. Naturally, 'liberal Islam' has its detractors: on the Muslim side there are those who denounce it as un-Islamic, while on the Western side there are those who reject as not being liberal enough.

Such criticisms echo the response given to the modernist reform movement of the early twentieth century, when Muslim reformers were denounced by their more traditionalist peers as 'dupes of Satan'. Yet if the 'house of Islam' is to survive and flourish in today's global village – and flourish from a position of strength and dignity – then it is clear that reform of some sort is desirable. As we enter the year 2000, replete with hopes and aspirations for all our futures, is it possible that 'liberal Islam' will have an important part to play in restoring to the Muslim world some of the good fortune witnessed in the 'golden age' of the Caliphate or the era of the great medieval Islamic empires? Time and time alone will tell.

Notes

1   The Arabic word *hadith* (lit. 'utterance'), usually translated into English as 'tradition', refers to the recorded reports of Muhammad's sayings or actions, compiled into six authoritative collections in the ninth century.

2   The Koran, ch. 96, v. 1–5.

3   A detailed exposition of the Islamic belief system as enshrined in the Koran is clearly beyond the scope of this book. For a lucid account of the fundamentals of faith and the pillars of belief, see Fazlur Rahman, *Islam* (London, 1966).

4   *ulama*, meaning 'those with knowledge', is the collective term for Muslim scholars, particularly those versed in the disciplines of *hadith* transmission and jurisprudence. It is sometimes translated erroneously into English as 'clergy', a concept which in theory does not exist in Muslim religious society.

5   The Ismailis, another offshoot of the Shi'ites, also believe that the guardianship of the Muslim community had been vested in a series of 'divinely guided' imams drawn from the family of the Prophet. They hold the first six imams in common with the Twelver Shi'ites, but differ with the latter on the question of succession to the sixth imam, hence their epithet 'The Seveners'. The notorious 'Order of the Assassins' were a militant offshoot of the Ismaili sect.

6   For example, the Seljuk sultanate of Rum, based in Konya from 1077 to 1307.

7   J.J. Saunders, *A History of Medieval Islam* (London, 1965), p. 181.

8   Roger Savory, 'Christendom v. Islam: Interaction and Co-existence', in *Introduction to Islamic Civilization*, Roger Savory, ed. (Cambridge, 1976), p. 133.

9   Vladimir Minorsky, 'Shaykh Bali Efendi on the Safavids', in

Bulletin of the School of Oriental and African Studies, vol. 20 (1957), p. 439.

10 The word 'Moghul' comes from the Persian word for Mongol; an alternative English rendering is Mughal.

11 The Hidden Imam, also known as the Mahdi, is the messianic figure who, according to the majority of Muslims, will come at the end of time to restore peace and justice to the world. Most Shi'ites believe that he is alive now, but in concealment or 'occultation'.

12 John L. Esposito, *Islam: The Straight Path* (Oxford, 1994), pp. 150–1.

Glossary

ansar The 'helpers' of Muhammad native to Medina, as distinct from the *muhajirun* who accompanied him on his flight from Mecca.

dar al-harb The 'abode of war', or those lands not under Muslim jurisdiction; also, any community or state hostile to Islam, and in which jihad against the forces of unbelief may legitimately be waged.

dar al-Islam The 'abode of Islam/peace', or those lands under Muslim jurisdiction; also, any community or state in which Muslims are free to implement Islam without let or hindrance.

devshirme The system of recruitment and training of Christian youths for military and administrative service implemented by the Ottoman *sultans*.

fiqh Islamic jurisprudence.

ghulat Adherents of *ghuluww* (see below); extremists.

ghuluww lit. 'exaggeration'; used to describe the mostly antinomian practices, mostly pro-Shi'ite in nature, of the Turkish nomads of eastern Anatolia in the thirteenth and fourteenth centuries, but also used to describe any doctrine or set of doctrines that is held by the orthodoxy to be beyond the pale of Islam.

hadith 'Tradition' or report of a saying or action of Muhammad.

hajj The pilgrimage to Mecca which every adult Muslim must make at least once in his or her lifetime.

hanif A term used to describe those Arabs who believed in the concept of one Creator, but who were neither Jews nor Christians, prior to the revelation of the Koran.

hijra The flight of Muhammad and his followers from Mecca to Medina in 622.

ijtihad The use of independent judgement, usually through analogical reasoning, to derive new legal rulings from the existing body of law.

GLOSSARY

imam lit. 'one who stands in front', hence 'prayer leader' or 'leader of the community'. In Shi'ite tradition, Ali and those of his descendants (e.g. the Twelve Imams) who are seen as the inheritors of Muhammad's spiritual and temporal authority and who thus have the right to rule the community.

jahiliyya The 'age of ignorance' prior to the revelation of the Koran and the advent of Islam.

jihad Defensive war against unbelievers. The word is also used to describe the personal struggle of the soul against its baser instincts.

jizya A form of poll tax levied on non-Muslim minorities under Muslim rule.

ka'ba Sacred cubic structure in Mecca which marks the direction of daily prayer and serves as the focus for the annual pilgrimage.

khalifa lit. 'deputy'; a term used to describe the early successors of the Prophet, usually anglicized as caliph.

khan Mongol word for 'lord', signifying the ruler of a state.

khanate A territory under the jurisdiction of a khan.

madhhab Rite or 'school' of jurisprudence.

mahdi lit. 'the guided one'; the messianic figure who, Muslims believe, will come at the end of time to restore peace and justice to the world.

millet A separate community within the Ottoman empire in which non-Muslim minorities were allowed to live in accordance with their own laws.

muhajirun lit. 'emigrants'; those who accompanied Muhammad on his flight from Mecca to Medina.

mujtahid Someone who practises *ijtihad*.

shah Persian for 'king' or 'emperor'; sometimes used interchangeably with *shahanshah*, which means 'king of kings'.

shari'a lit. 'the path to a water hole'; the name given to the body of Islamic laws derived from the Koran and the *sunna*.

shaykh lit. 'elder'; the chief of a tribe; a Sufi master, but also used as an honorific title for any religious leader.

shi'a The 'party' of Ali, initially comprising those Muslims in Medina who championed Ali's right to succeed the Prophet as temporal and spiritual leader of the community.

sufi An adherent of Sufism, or Islamic mysticism.

sultan lit. 'authority'; this term was first used in the tenth century to denote the actual holder of power in society, as distinct from the *khalifa*, and hence became as the normal Muslim term for sovereign.

sunna The 'custom' or 'practice' of Muhammad, as enshrined in the Traditions.

Tanzimat The westernizing reforms initiated by the Ottoman *sultans* in the nineteenth century.

ulama lit. 'those with knowledge'; the collective term for Muslim scholars, particularly those versed in the disciplines of hadith transmission and jurisprudence.

umma The Muslim community.

zakat The fixed tax on income and capital (normally 2.5 per cent) payable at the end of every financial year for charitable purchases.

Further Reading

GENERAL REFERENCE WORKS ON ISLAM

The standard work of reference for any subject to do with Islam or Islamic civilization is the monumental *Encyclopaedia of Islam* (eds. J.H. Kramers *et al*, 2nd edition, Leiden, 1954–). All entries carry extensive bibliographies. To consult it, however, you need to know the Arabic term for the subject you are looking for; the system of transliteration also leaves much to be desired. These quibbles aside, it is an outstanding work, and a fitting tribute to almost half a century of outstanding Western scholarship on Islam.

For the interested layman, general introductory works on Islam abound, although they differ greatly in quality. One of the most readable, and least sensational, introductions to the emergence of the Islamic community, the doctrines of Islam, the question of tradition versus modernity, and the resurgence of Islam in the twentieth century is J.L. Esposito, *Islam: The Straight Path* (Oxford University Press, 1994), with M. Ruthven, *Islam in the World* (Penguin, London, 1991) a close second.

THE PROPHET

The standard western work on Muhammad's life and career is W. Montgomery Watt, *Muhammad: Prophet and Statesman* (London, 1961), an extremely detailed and meticulously researched piece of scholarship. A much shorter and possibly more digestible alternative is M. Cook, *Muhammad* (Oxford University Press, 1996). Those interested enough to tackle it may like to try A. Guillaume's translation of Ibn Ishaq, *The Life of Muhammad* (London, 1955), the earliest known biography of the Prophet, written in the middle of the eighth century.

THE FIRST NINE CENTURIES (632–1500)

For detailed general histories of part or all of the first nine centuries of Islamic history, readers are best served by J.J. Saunders, *A History of Medieval Islam* (London, 1965), E.G. von Grunebaum, *Classical Islam: History 600–1258* (Allen & Unwin, London, 1970) and, above all, M.G.S. Hodgson, *The Venture of Islam* (3 vols., University of Chicago Press, 1974), which gives excellent coverage of the whole period. F. Donner, *Early Islamic Conquests* (Cambridge, Mass., 1982) offers a fascinating insight into the causes and consequences of the Arab conquests. A. Cheyne, *Muslim Spain: Its History and Culture* (Minnesota, 1974) and C.P. Harvey, *Islamic Spain 1250–1500* (London, 1990) provide readable coverage of Islamic Spain, while C. Hillenbrand, *The Crusades: Islamic Perspectives* (Edinburgh University Press, 1999), meticulously researched and lavishly illustrated, is the definitive work on the Crusades from the Muslim viewpoint.

Readers with an interest in the nature and development of the Islamic world of learning in this period should begin with I. Goldziher, *Introduction to Islamic Theology and Law*, translated by A. and R. Hamori (Princeton University Press, 1981) for coverage of law and theology, and M. Fakhry, *A History of Islamic Philosophy* (Longman, London & New York, 1983) for the history of Islamic philosophy. The development of Sufism is charted in J.S. Trimingham, *The Sufi Orders in Islam* (Oxford University Press, 1971), while two excellent studies of Shi'ism and other 'heterodox' movements exist in M. Momen, *An Introduction to Shi'i Islam: the History and Doctrines of Twelver Shi'ism* (London, 1985) and H. Halm, *Shi'ism*, translated by J. Watson (Edinburgh University Press, 1991).

THE OTTOMANS, SAFAVIDS AND MOGHULS

H. Inalcik, *The Ottoman Empire: The Classical Age 1300–1600* (Weidenfeld & Nicolson, London, 1973) is the standard academic work on the 'glory years' of the Ottoman empire, while R. Savory, *Iran under the Safavids* (Cambridge University Press, 1980) deals with the rise and fall of the Safavids with a clarity matched by no other Safavid historian. The definitive work on Moghul India remains to be written, although newcomers to the subject could do worse than to begin with B. Gascoigne, *The Great Moghuls* (Cape, London, 1971), which is both well illustrated and lucidly written. F. Robinson, *Atlas of the Islamic World since 1500* (Oxford & New York, 1982) offers an excellent general overview of the decline of the three empires, while one of the best introductions to the concept of revivalism can be found in F. Rahman, *Islam* (London, 1966).

COLONIALISM AND REFORM IN THE EIGHTEENTH AND NINETEENTH CENTURIES

Apart from the general titles already mentioned, there are few comprehensive studies of the Muslim response to the rise of European rule and the modern state. N.R. Keddie (ed.), *Scholars, Saints and Sufis: Muslim Religious Institutions since 1500* (University of California Press, Berkeley, 1972) is a collection of articles covering most of the Muslim Middle East and North Africa, while A. Hourani, *Arabic Thought In The Liberal Age, 1798–1935* (London, 1962) is a penetrating study of the emergence, in response to European domination, of Arab nationalist thought.

ISLAM IN THE TWENTIETH CENTURY

For a general account of the interplay between Islam and politics, E. Mortimer, *Faith and Power: The Politics of Islam* (London, 1982) is a good starting point. J. Piscatori (ed.), *Islam in the Political Process*

(Cambridge University Press, 1983) is an excellent collection of articles that deal with the various manifestations of political Islam in different parts of the Muslim world, while M.J. Fischer, *Iran: From Religious Dispute to Revolution* (Harvard University Press, Cambridge, Mass., 1980) provides a compelling study of Islam as the vehicle for sociopolitical revolution, in this case in Iran. For well-researched accounts of the evolution, structure and objectives of the principal Islamist movements, G. Kepel, *The Prophet and Pharaoh: Muslim Extremism in Egypt* (Al Saqi Books, London, 1985), S.V.R. Nasr, *The Vanguard of Islamic Revolution: The Jama'at-i Islami of Pakistan* (University of California Press, Berkeley, 1994) and S. Taji-Farouki, *A Fundamental Quest* (Grey Seal Books, London, 1996) are recommended.

Index

Bold type indicates main or more significant entries.

112